The Complete Guitar Player Rock Songbook

Published by:
Wise Publications
14-15 Berners Street, London W1T 3LJ, UK.

Exclusive Distributors:
Music Sales Limited
Distribution Centre, Newmarket Road, Bury St Edmunds, Suffolk IP33 3YB, UK.
Music Sales Corporation
180 Madison Avenue, 24th Floor, New York NY 10016, USA.
Music Sales Pty Limited
Units 3-4, 17 Willfox Street, Condell Park, NSW 2200, Australia.

Compiled and edited by Toby Knowles.
Music processed by shedwork.com.
Cover designed by Fresh Lemon.
Printed in the EU.

The Complete
Guitar Player
Rock
Songbook

Wise Publications
part of The Music Sales Group
London / New York / Paris / Sydney / Copenhagen / Berlin / Madrid / Hong Kong / Tokyo

All Day And All Of The Night

Words & Music by Ray Davies

The strumming rhythm shown in the intro should be played with solid, detached down-strums. Play it in the verse, too, before a freer feel for the chorus.

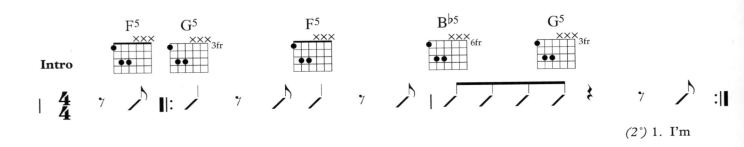

Chorus

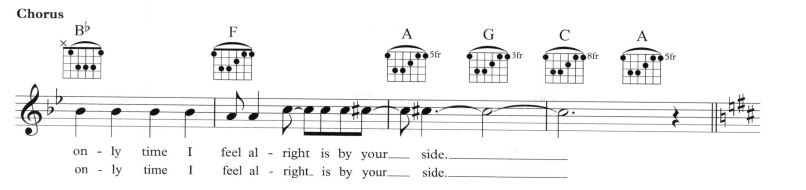

on - ly time I feel al - right is by your___ side._____
on - ly time I feel al - right_ is by your___ side._____

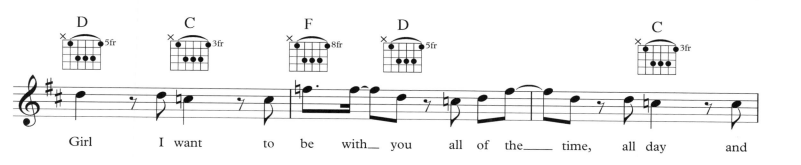

Girl I want to be with___ you all of the___ time, all day and

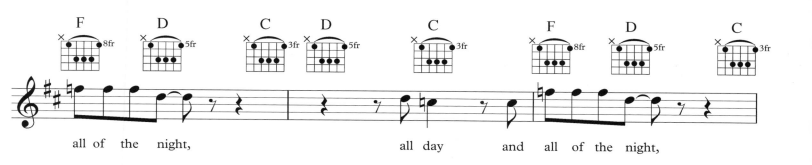

all of the night, all day and all of the night,

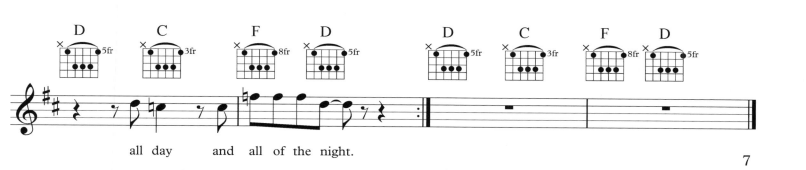

all day and all of the night.

All Right Now

Words & Music by Paul Rodgers & Andy Fraser

Strumming style:

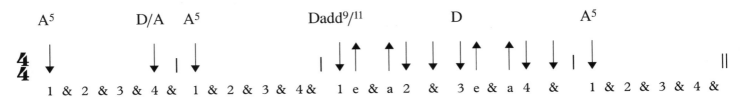

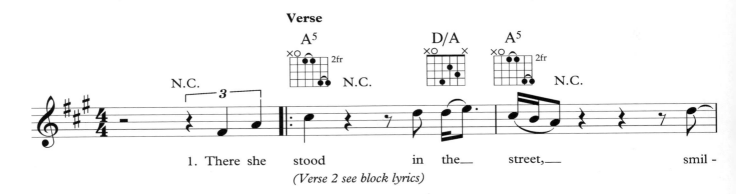

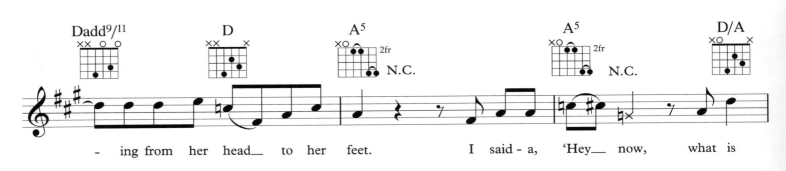

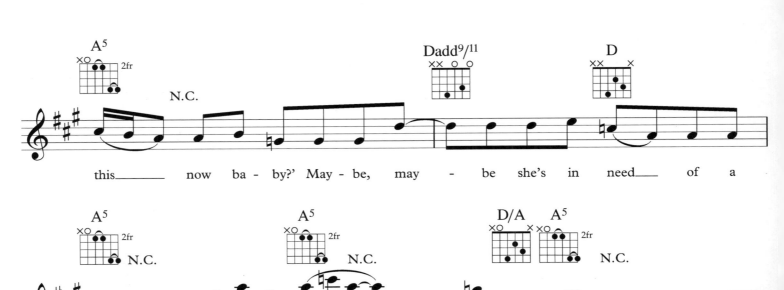

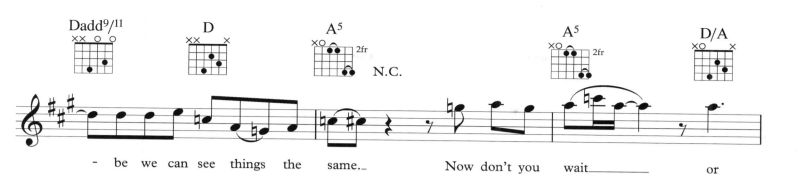

- be we can see things the same._ Now don't you wait_____ or

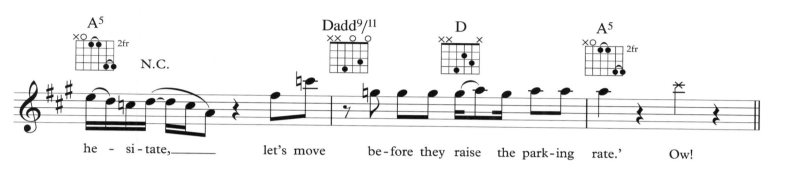

he - si - tate,_____ let's move be-fore they raise the park-ing rate.' Ow!

Chorus

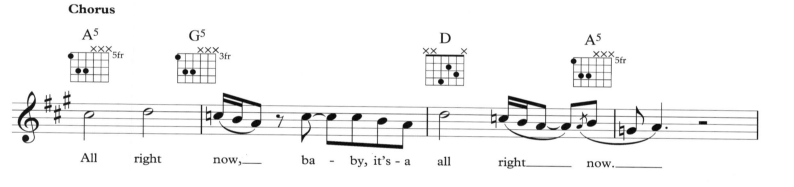

All right now,___ ba - by, it's - a all right_____ now._____

1.

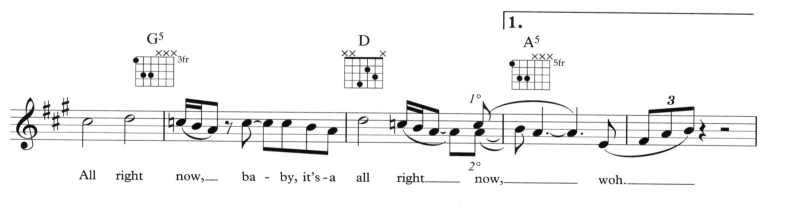

All right now,___ ba - by, it's - a all right_____ now,_____ woh._____

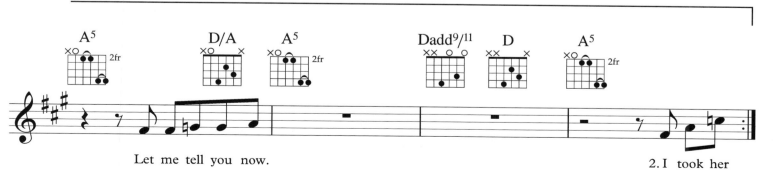

Let me tell you now.   2. I took her

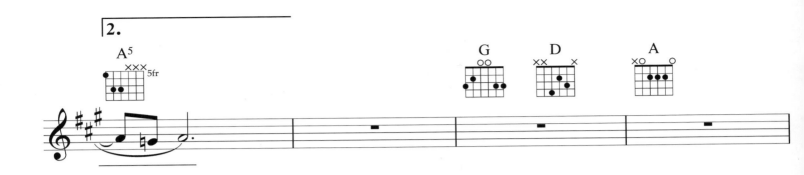

Guitar Solo

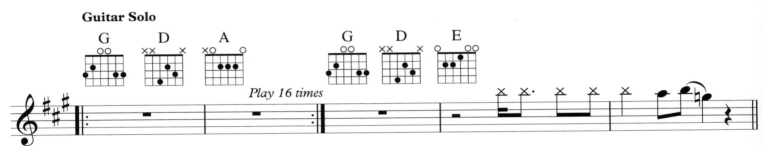

Play 16 times

I said, don't you know. Oh, yeah.

Outro

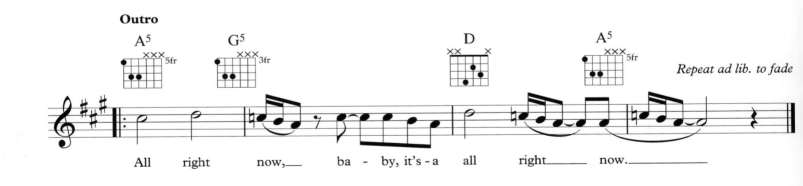

Repeat ad lib. to fade

All right now,___ ba - by, it's - a all right___ now._____

Verse 2:
I took her home to my place,
Watchin' every move on her face.
She said 'Look, what's your game, baby?
Are you try'n' to put me in shame?'

I said-a, 'Slow, don't go so fast,
Don't you think that love can last?'
She said, 'Love, Lord above,
Now you're try'n' to trick me in love.'

Alone

Words & Music by Tom Kelly & Billy Steinberg

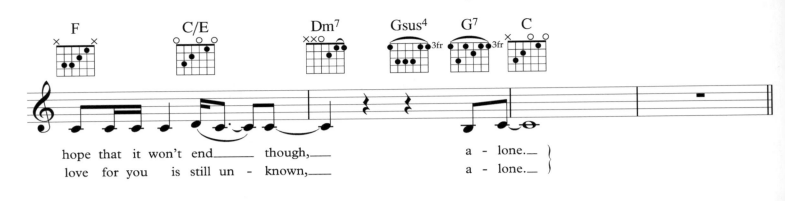

hope that it won't end_____ though,____
love for you is still un - known,____
a - lone.__
a - lone.__

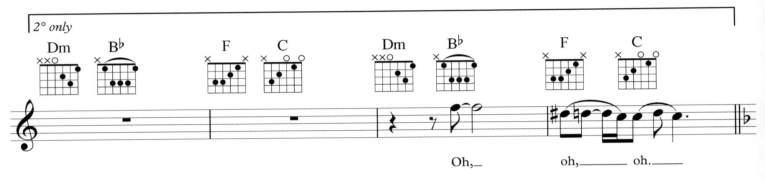

2° only

Oh,__ oh,_____ oh.__

Chorus

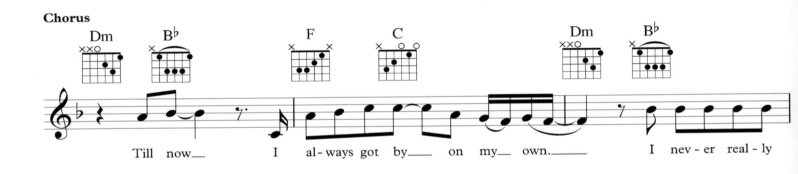

Till now__ I al-ways got by__ on my__ own.__ I nev-er real-ly

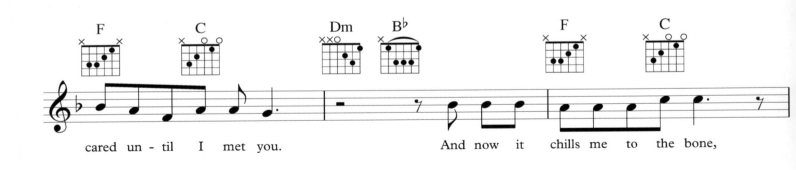

cared un - til I met you. And now it chills me to the bone,

1.

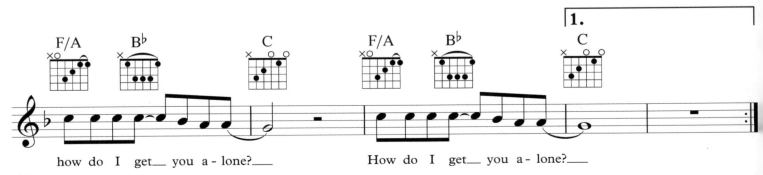

how do I get__ you a - lone?____ How do I get__ you a - lone?____

Crazy Little Thing Called Love

Words & Music by Freddie Mercury

Intro riff:

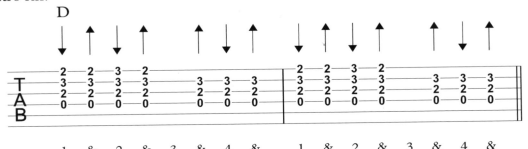

Intro

This thing____ called love____ I just____

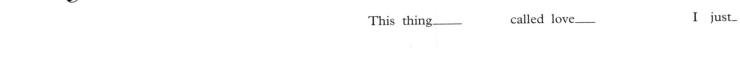

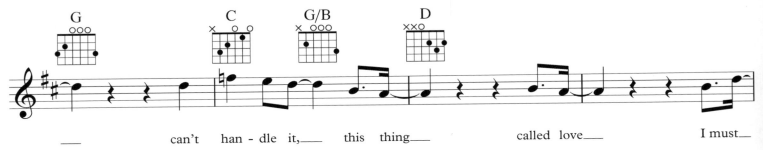

____ can't han - dle it,____ this thing____ called love____ I must____

To Coda

—— get round to it,____ I ain't read - y. Cra - zy lit - tle thing called love,

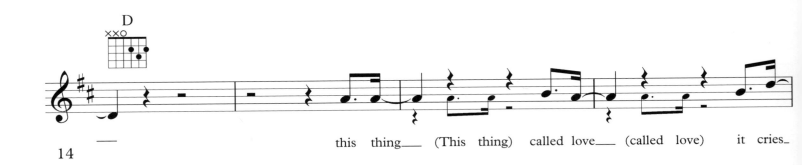

——— this thing____ (This thing) called love____ (called love) it cries____

— (like a ba - by) in a cra - dle all night,_ it swings_ (woo woo) it jives_

— (woo woo) it shakes all o - ver like a jel - ly - fish__ I kind - a

like it   Cra - zy lit - tle thing called love.__   There goes my

Bridge

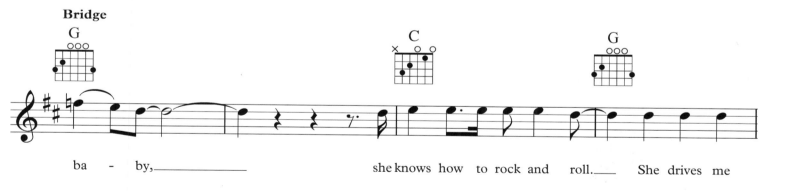

ba - by,_____   she knows how to rock and roll.__ She drives me

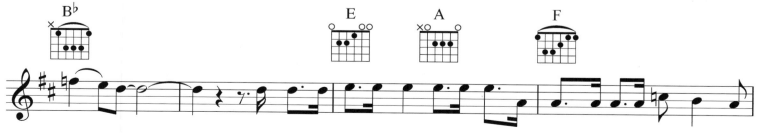

cra - zy_____   she gives me hot and cold fe - ver, then she leaves me in a cool, cool sweat.

15

I got - ta be cool___ re - lax,___ get hip,_

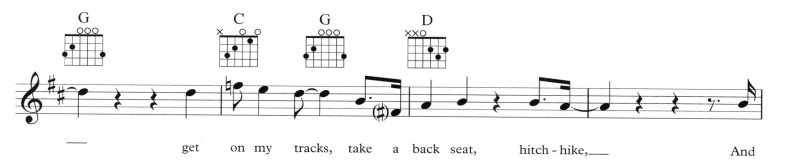

___ get on my tracks, take a back seat, hitch - hike,___ And

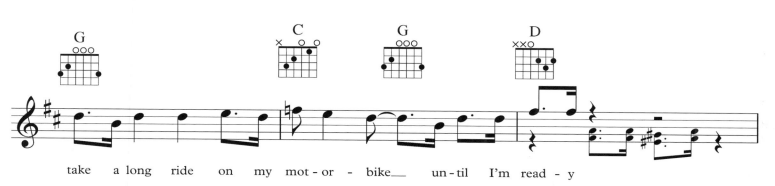

take a long ride on my mot - or - bike___ un - til I'm read - y

(rea - dy Fred - die)

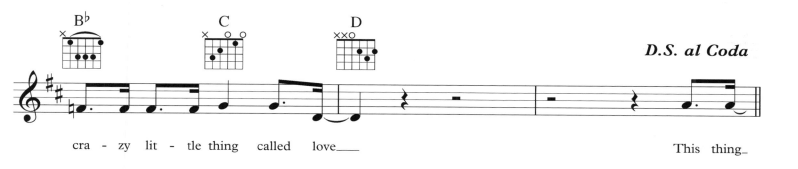

cra - zy lit - tle thing called love___ This thing_

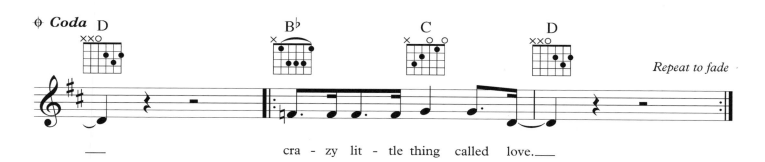

___ cra - zy lit - tle thing called love.___

Born To Be Wild

Words & Music by Mars Bonfire

Strumming style:

Intro

Verse

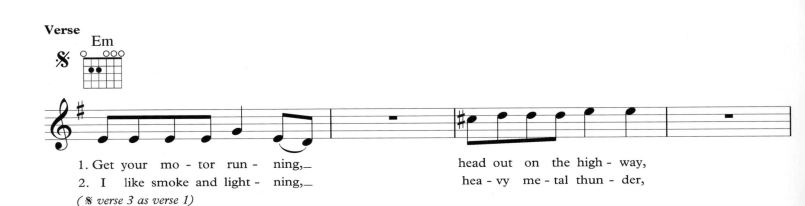

1. Get your mo - tor run - ning,__ head out on the high - way,
2. I like smoke and light - ning,__ hea - vy me - tal thun - der,

(℅ verse 3 as verse 1)

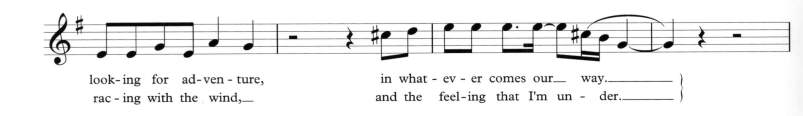

look-ing for ad-ven-ture, in what-ev-er comes our__ way._____
rac-ing with the wind,__ and the feel-ing that I'm un-der._____

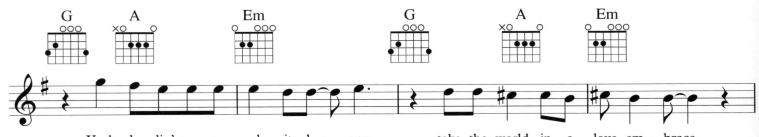

Yeah dar-lin' gon-na make it hap-pen, take the world in a love em-brace,

19

Call Me

Words by Deborah Harry
Music by Giorgio Moroder

Strumming style:

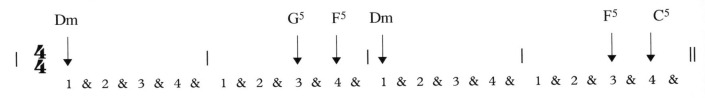

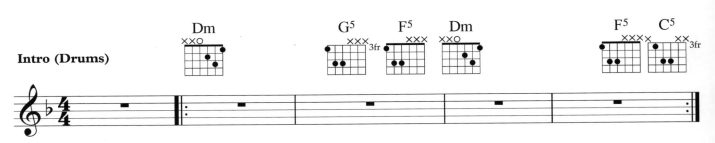

Intro (Drums)

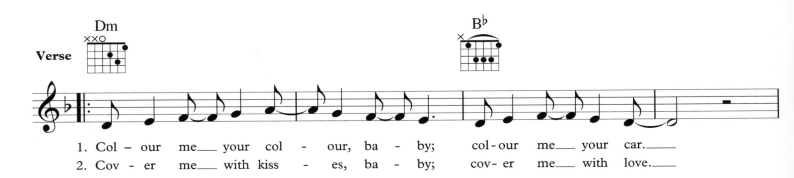

1. Col - our me___ your col - our, ba - by; col-our me___ your car.
2. Cov - er me___ with kiss - es, ba - by; cov - er me___ with love.___

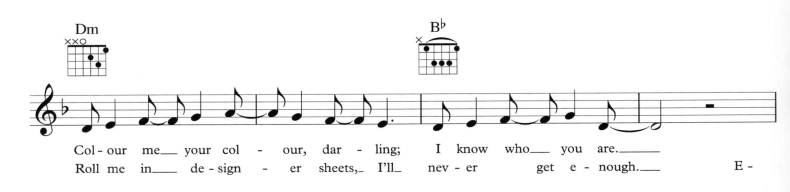

Col - our me___ your col - our, dar - ling; I know who___ you are.___
Roll me in___ de - sign - er sheets,_ I'll_ nev - er get e - nough.___ E -

1° only

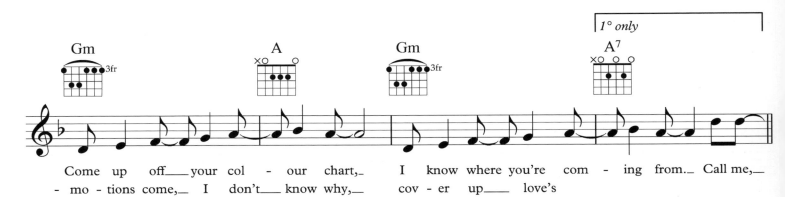

Come up off___your col - our chart,_ I know where you're com - ing from.__ Call me,
- mo - tions come,_ I don't___ know why,_ cov - er up___ love's

20

21

Call me,

Chorus

my love;___ call me, call me an-y, an-y-time.__ Call

me, for a ride;___ call me, call me for some o-ver-time.__ Call

me, my love;___ call me, call me in a sweet de-sign.__ Call

me, call me for your lov-er's lov-er's al-i-bi.__ Call

me on the line,__ call me, call me an-y, an-y-time.__ Call

Repeat and fade

me! Oh, call me, ooh,__ ooh,__ ah.__ Call

Chasing Cars

Words & Music by Paul Wilson, Gary Lightbody, Jonathan Quinn, Nathan Connolly & Tom Simpson

Chorus

here,
if I just lay here,—
would you lie

1.
with me— and— just for-get the world?——

2.
For-get what we're told——

be-fore we get too old.—
Show me a

gar-den— that's burst-ing in-to life.—

Verse

3. Let's waste— time— chas-ing— cars—

— a-round—— our— heads.—

25

Cocaine

Words & Music by J.J. Cale

This entire song can be played with a single barred shape using just one finger! It's how J.J. Cale played it himself. Add a little crunchy overdrive, and you're good to go!

Intro

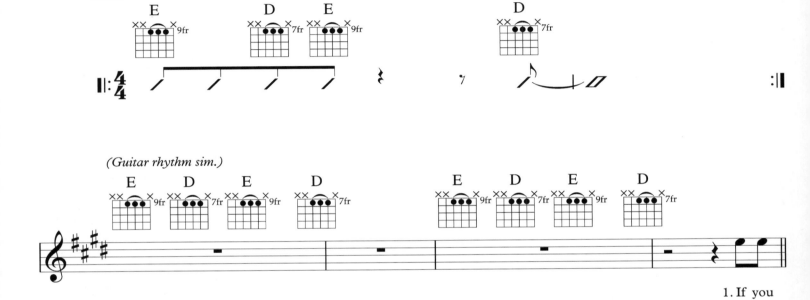

1. If you

Verse

wan - na hang out, you got to take her out;__ co - caine.__
(2.) got bad__ news, you wan - na kick them blues; co - caine.__
(3.) thing__ is gone and you wan - na ride on; co - caine.__

If you wan - na get down, down on the ground; co - caine.
When your day is__ done and you wan - na__ run; co - caine.
Don't for - get this__ fact: you can't get__ back; co - caine.

Black

Words by Eddie Vedder
Music by Stone Gossard

It's enough to play a single chord per bar for this song, allowing it
to ring on. Create a dense, dark sound with distortion and a little
reverb. For the chorus, try constant eighth-note down-strums.

1. Sheets of emp-ty can-vas,_ un-touched sheets of clay_ were

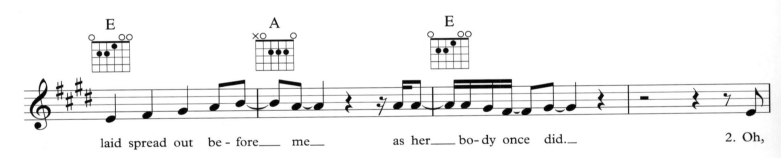

laid spread out be-fore_ me_ as her_ bo-dy once did._ 2. Oh,

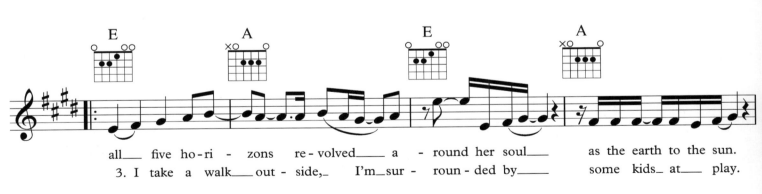

all_ five ho-ri-zons re-volved_ a-round her soul_ as the earth to the sun.
3. I take a walk_ out-side,_ I'm_sur-roun-ded by_ some kids_ at_ play.

Now the air I tas-ted and breathed has_ ta-ken a turn._ Ooh,
I can feel their laugh-ter,_ so why do I sear? Ooh,

Outro

Repeat to fade

Creep

Words & Music by Albert Hammond, Mike Hazlewood, Thom Yorke,
Jonny Greenwood, Colin Greenwood, Ed O'Brien & Phil Selway

Picking pattern:

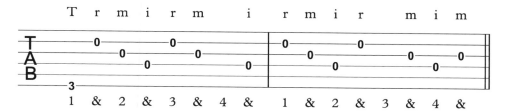

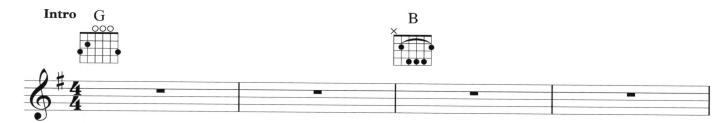

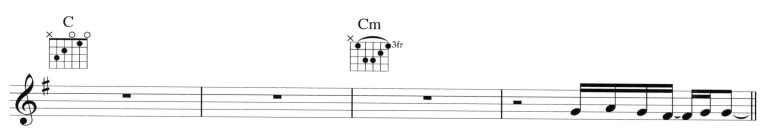

1. When you were here_ be-fore,_

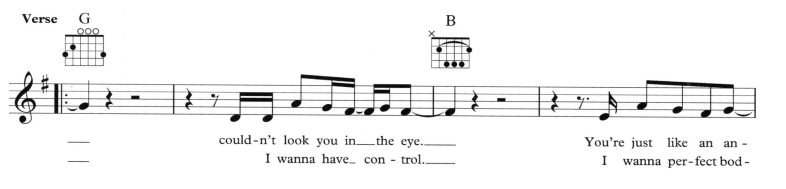

could-n't look you in___the eye._____ You're just like an an -
I wanna have_ con - trol.____ I wanna per-fect bod -

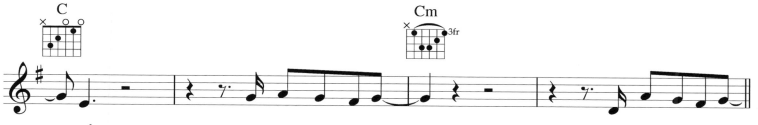

- gel,   your skin makes me cry._____   You float like a feath -
- y,   I wanna per - fect soul._____   I want you to no -

33

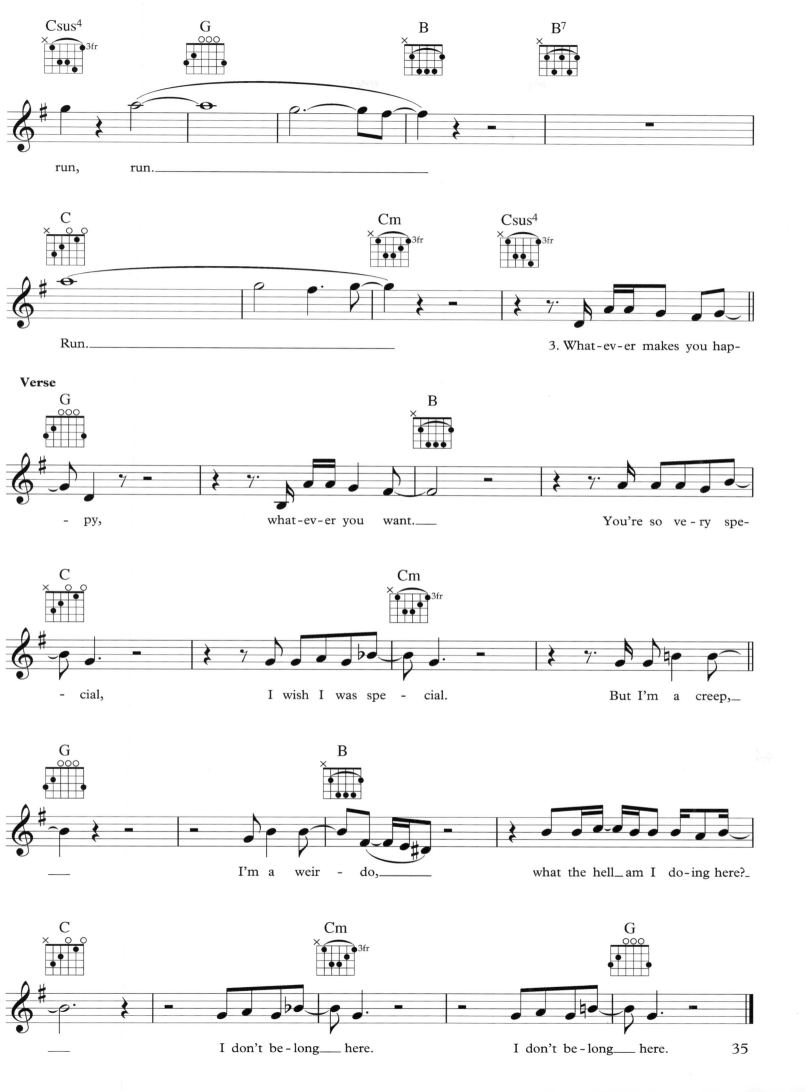

run, run.

Run.   3. What-ev-er makes you hap-

Verse

- py,   what-ev-er you want.   You're so ve-ry spe-

- cial,   I wish I was spe - cial.   But I'm a creep,

—   I'm a weir - do,   what the hell am I do-ing here?

—   I don't be-long here.   I don't be-long here.

Don't Look Back In Anger

Words & Music by Noel Gallagher

Picking style:

1. Slip in - side___ the eye of your mind,_____ don't you know you might find___
2. Take me to___ the place where you go,_____ where___ no - bod - y knows___

a bet - ter place to play._____
if it's night or day._____

You said___ that you'd___ ne - ver been,_____ but all the things that you've seen___
Please don't put your life___ in my hands_____ of a___ Rock 'n' Roll band.___

will slow - ly fade a - way.___
who'll throw it all a - way.___

So I start a re-vo-lu-tion from my bed, 'cause you

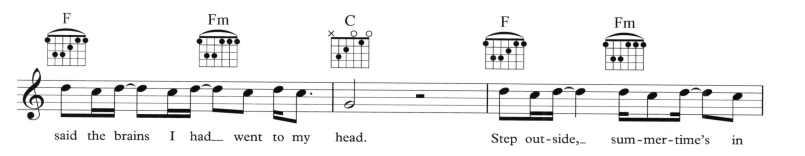

said the brains I had went to my head. Step out-side, sum-mer-time's in

bloom, stand up be-side the fire - place, take that look from off your face,

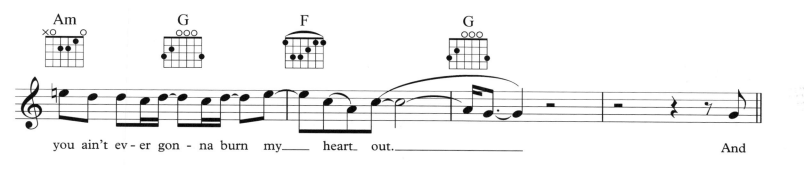

you ain't ev-er gon-na burn my heart out. And

Chorus

so Sal-ly can wait, she knows it's too late as we're walk-ing on by.

37

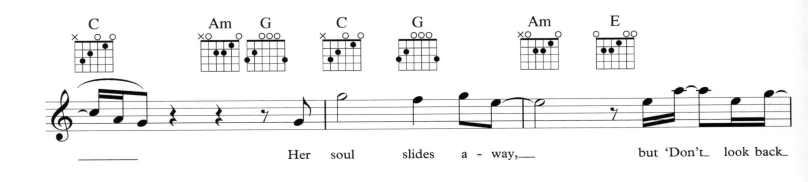

Her soul slides a-way,___ but 'Don't_ look back_

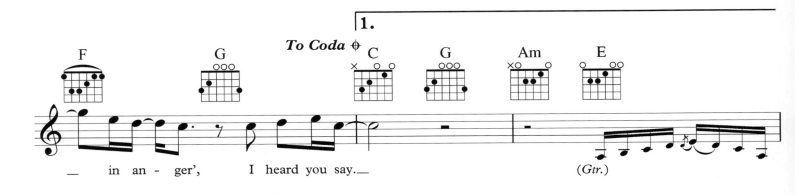

1.

To Coda ⊕

_ in an-ger', I heard you say.___ *(Gtr.)*

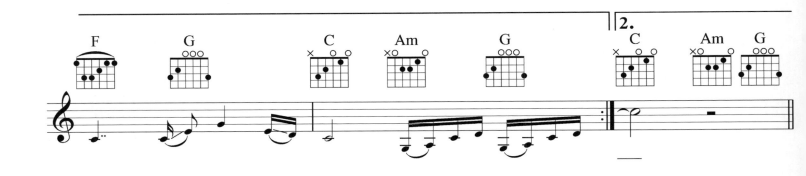

2.

Guitar Solo

F   Fm   C   F   Fm   C

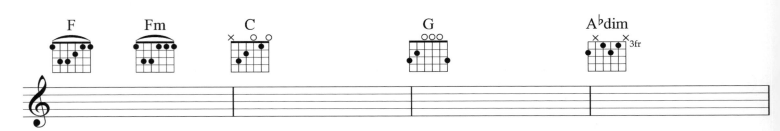

F   Fm   C   G   A♭dim

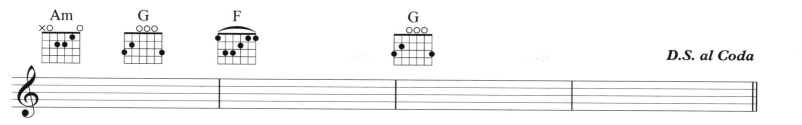

D.S. al Coda

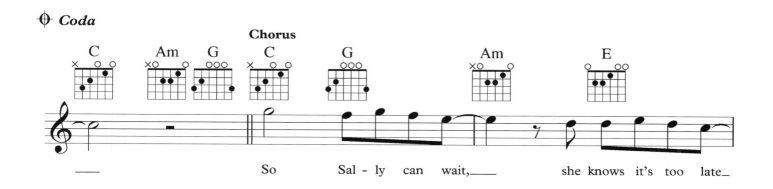

⊕ Coda

Chorus

So Sal - ly can wait,___ she knows it's too late___

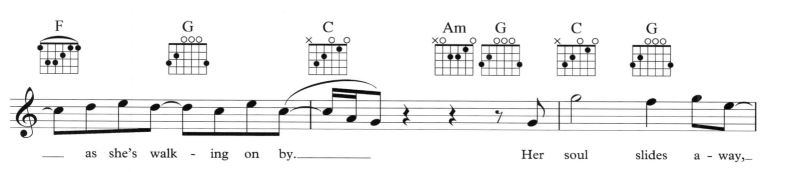

___ as she's walk - ing on by._____ Her soul slides a - way,___

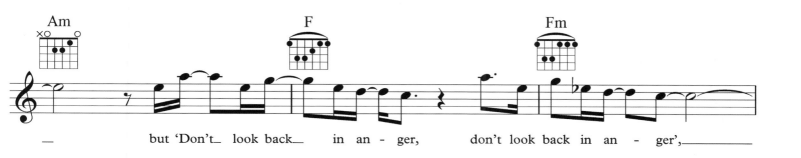

___ but 'Don't___ look back___ in an - ger, don't look back in an - ger',_____

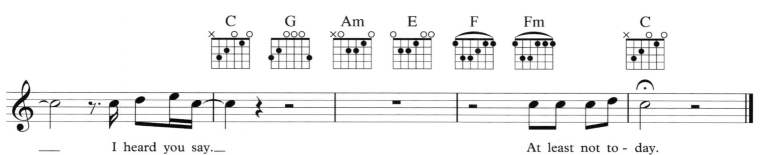

___ I heard you say.___ At least not to - day.

39

Eye Of The Tiger

Words & Music by Jim Peterik & Frank Sullivan III

A second guitar can play the constant sixteenth-notes shown below throughout the intro and verses. Aim for a detached, steady pulse to accompany the main rhythm part.

41

Face to face— out in the heat.———— Hang-in' tough, stay-in'

hun - gry. They stack the odds still we take to the street for the kill,—

— with the skill to sur - vive.—— It's—— the

2.

Verse

N.C.

tig - er. 2. Ri - sin' up,—

straight to the top.— Had the guts, got the glo - ry, Went the di - stance, now I'm

D.S. al Coda

not gon - na stop, just a man— with his will to sur-vive.—— It's— the

42

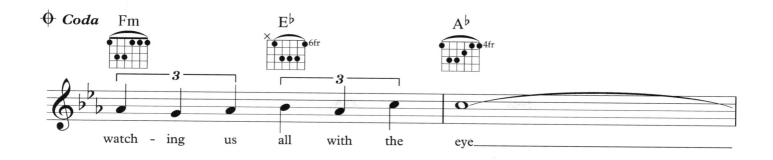

watch - ing us all with the eye_____

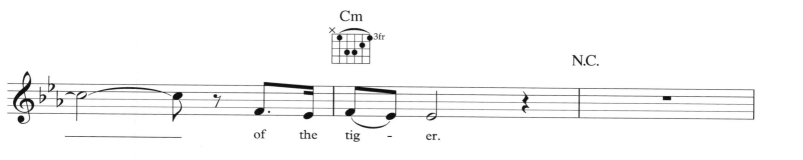

_____ of the tig - er.

Outro

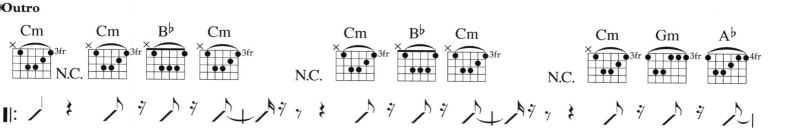

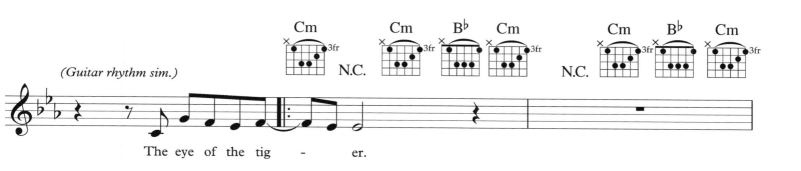

(Guitar rhythm sim.)

The eye of the tig - er.

Repeat to fade

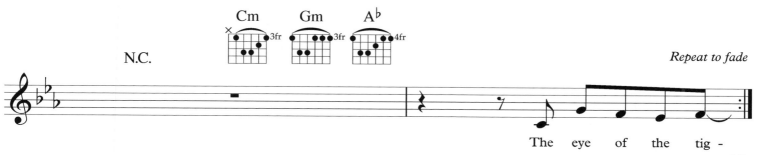

The eye of the tig -

Every Breath You Take

Words & Music by Sting

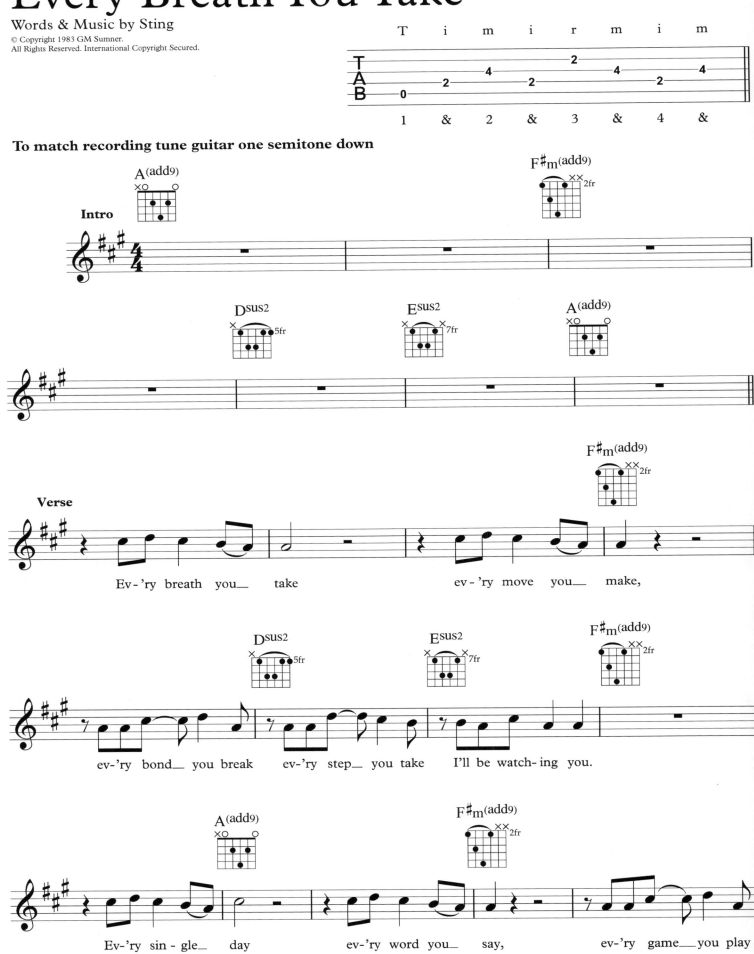

To match recording tune guitar one semitone down

- ly see__ your face, I look a-round but it's you I can't__ re-place, I feel so cold and I

long for your__ em- brace. I keep cry- ing ba - by ba - by please.__

A(add9)   **F**♯**m**(add9)   **D**sus2

Esus2   **A**(add9)   *D.S. al Coda*

Oh can't you__

⊕ *Coda*

F♯**m**(add9)   **D**sus2   **E**sus2   **F**♯**m**(add9)

Ev-'ry move__you make ev-'ry step__ you take, I'll be watch-ing you.

A(add9)   **F**♯**m**(add9)   **D**sus2

Repeat ad. lib to fade

I'll be watch-ing you.__   I'll be watch-ing

The Final Countdown

Words & Music by Joey Tempest

If you are playing this with another guitarist, one of you could try working out the original keyboard melody. The first few bars are shown in the TAB below.

Verse

1. We're leav-ing__ to-ge-ther, but still it's__ fare-well.__
2. We're head-ing__ for Ve-nus and still we__ stand__ tall.__

And may-be__ we'll come back__ to Earth.__ Who can tell?__
'Cause may-be__ they've seen us_____ and wel - come us all.__

I guess there is no one__ to blame. We're leav-ing ground.__ (leav-ing
With so ma-ny light years to go and things to be found__ (to be

ground)__ Will things e - ver be_____ the same a - gain? It's the fi - nal
found)__ I'm sure that__ we'll all_____ miss her so.

Chorus

count - down,_____ the fi - nal

1.

48 count - down._____

Here I Go Again

Words & Music by David Coverdale & Bernie Marsden

Chorus strumming style:

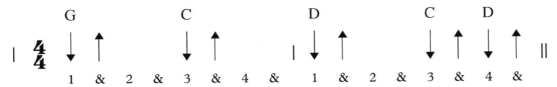

Intro

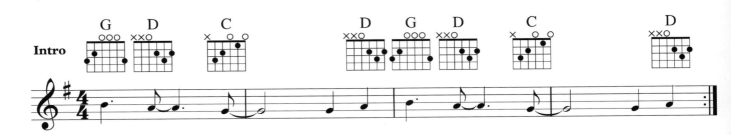

Verse

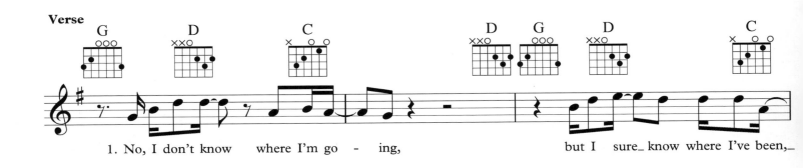

1. No, I don't know where I'm go - ing, but I sure_ know where I've been,_

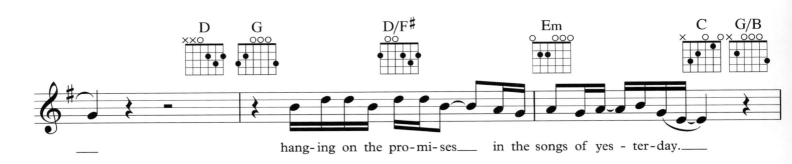

_ hang - ing on the pro - mi - ses_ in the songs of yes - ter - day._

And I've made up my mind:_ I ain't was - ting no more time._

2. Though I keep sear - ching for an ans - wer,
3. I'm just a-nother heart in need of re - scue,

I ne - ver seem to find what I'm look - ing for.
wait-ing on love's sweet cha - ri - ty._____

Oh Lord,_ I pray._ You give_ me strength_ to car - ry on_____
And I'm_ gon - na_ hold on_ for the_____ rest of_ my days,_____

'cause I know what it means_____ to walk a-long_ the lone-ly street_ of

Chorus

dreams. And here I go_ a-gain_ on my own,_____ go-ing

down the on - ly road_ I've e-ver known._____ Like a drif-ter I was born_ to walk a-lone._

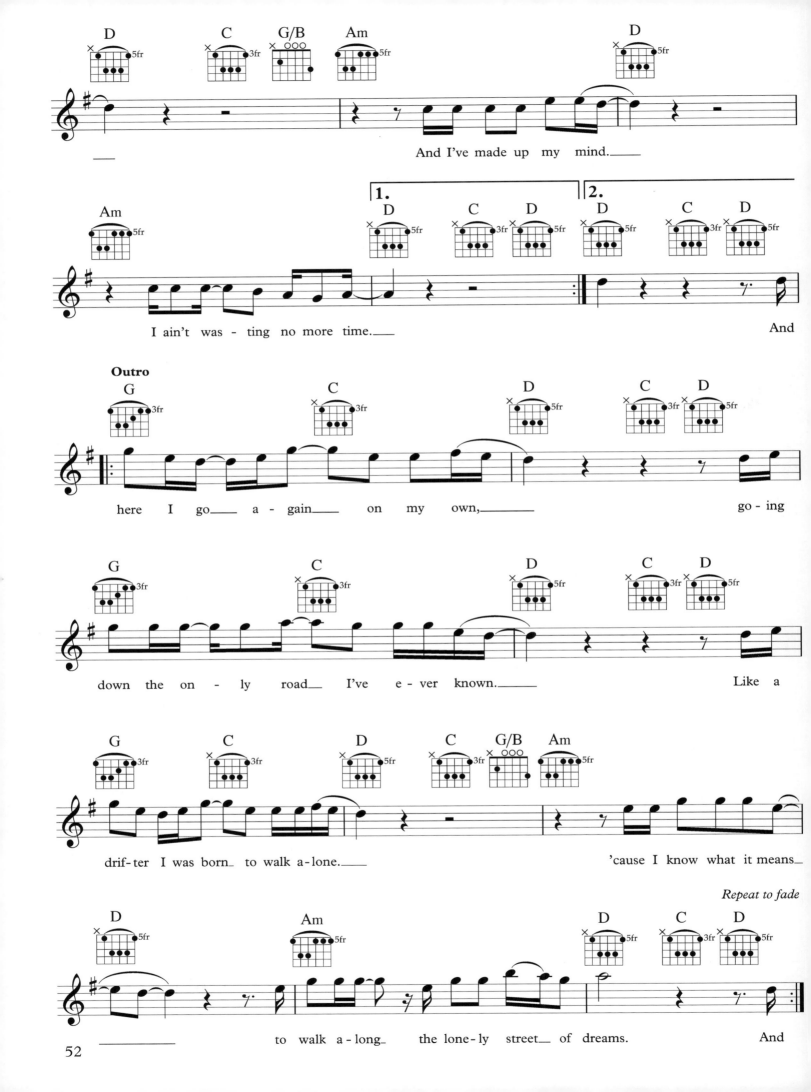

And I've made up my mind._____

1. **2.**

I ain't was - ting no more time._____ And

Outro

here I go_____ a - gain_____ on my own,_____ go - ing

down the on - ly road___ I've e - ver known._____ Like a

drif - ter I was born_ to walk a - lone._____ 'cause I know what it means_____

Repeat to fade

to walk a - long_ the lone - ly street___ of dreams. And

52

Heroes

Words by David Bowie
Music by David Bowie & Brian Eno

In the strumming rhythm below, the larger arrows show accented strums while the smaller ones are played softly.

Strumming style:

Intro

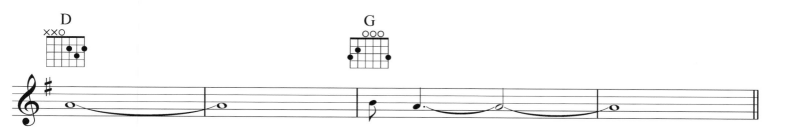

1. I,   I wish you could swim,____
2. I,   I will be king.____

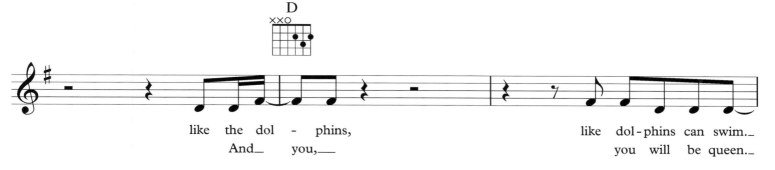

like the dol - phins,   like dol - phins can swim.__
And__ you,__   you will be queen.__

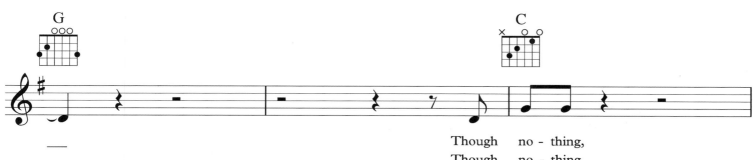

Though no - thing,
Though no - thing

- bove our heads. (Ov - er our_____ heads)   And we kissed_____

as though no-thing could fall.___   (No - thing could fall)_____   And the shame__

___   was on the oth-er side.   Oh we can beat__

__ them   for ev - er and ev - er,   then we could be He-

- roes   just for one day.___

Repeat to fade

We can be He - roes.

55

Hey Joe

Words & Music by Billy Roberts

Verse 2:
Uh, hey Joe, I heard you shot your woman down,
You shot her down now.
Uh, hey Joe, I heard you shot your old lady down,
You shot her down in the ground, yeah.
Yes, I did, I shot her,
You know I caught her messin' 'round, messin' 'round town.
Yes, I did, I shot her,
You know I caught my old lady messin' 'round town,
And I gave her the gun, I shot her!

Highway To Hell

Words & Music by Angus Young, Malcolm Young & Bon Scott

To match recording tune guitar one semitone down

I Don't Want To Miss A Thing

Words & Music by Diane Warren

Intro B⁷sus⁴   A/C♯   Esus⁴   *Play 4 times*

(4°) 1. I could

Verse D   A/C♯   Bm⁷

stay a-wake   just to hear you breath-ing,   watch you
(2.) close to you,   feel-ing your heart beat-ing,   and I'm

G   D/F♯   Em⁷

smile while you are sleep-ing, while you're far a-way and dream-ing. I could
won-d'ring what you're dream-ing, won-d'ring if it's me you're see-ing. Then I

D   A/C♯   Bm⁷

spend my life in this sweet sur-ren-der. I could
kiss your eyes and thank God we're to-geth-er. I just wan-na

1° only

G   D/F♯   Em⁷

stay lost in this mo-ment for-ev-er.   Ev-'ry mo-ment

62

miss one kiss. I just wan-na be with you,__ right here__ with you,__

just like this. I just wan-na hold__ you close,_____ feel your heart so

close to mine,_____ and just stay here in__ this mo-ment for all the

rest of time.__ Ba — by, ba — by.____

Chorus

Don't wan-na close_ my eyes,_ don't wan-na fall__ a-sleep, _'cause I'd

miss you, ba-by, and I don't wan-na miss a thing.__ 'Cause ev-en when I dream of you,__

64

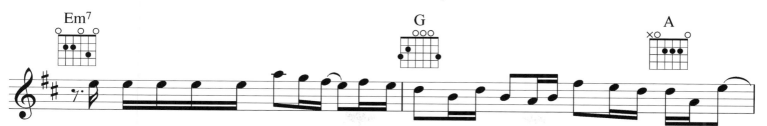

the sweet-est dream would nev-er do.__ I'd still miss you, ba-by, and I don't wan-na miss a thing.__

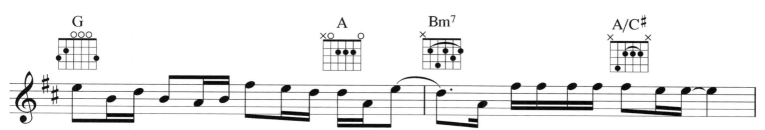

__ Don't wan-na close__ my eyes,__ don't wan-na fall__ a-sleep,__'cause I'd

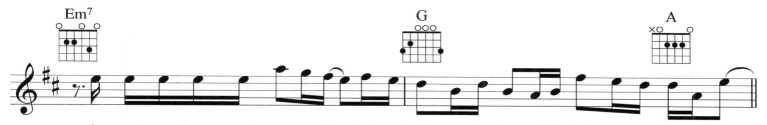

miss you, ba-by, and I don't wan-na miss a thing.__ 'Cause ev-en when I dream of you,__

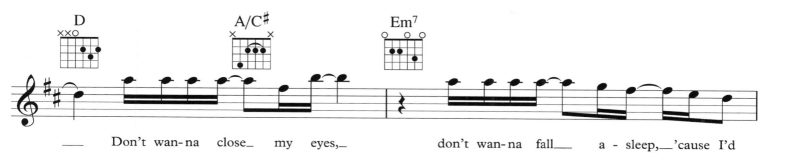

the sweet-est dream would nev-er do.__ I'd still miss you, ba-by, and I don't wan-na miss a thing.__

Outro

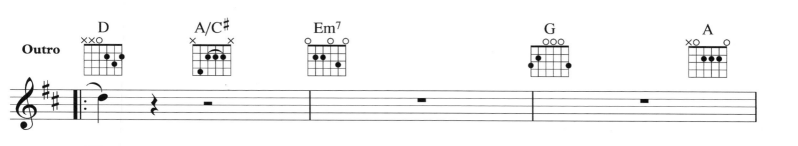

Repeat ad lib. to fade

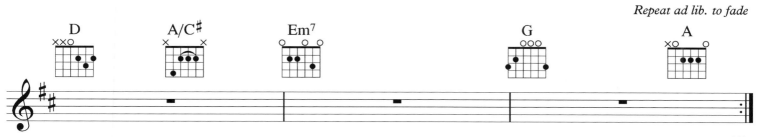

I Saw Her Standing There

Words & Music by John Lennon & Paul McCartney

Intro riff:

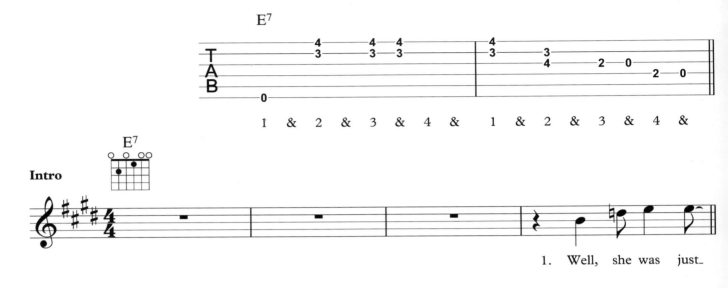

Intro

1. Well, she was just_

Verse

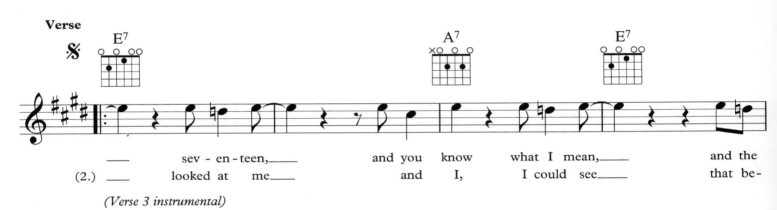

sev - en - teen,____ and you know what I mean,____ and the

(2.) ___ looked at me____ and I, I could see____ that be-

(Verse 3 instrumental)

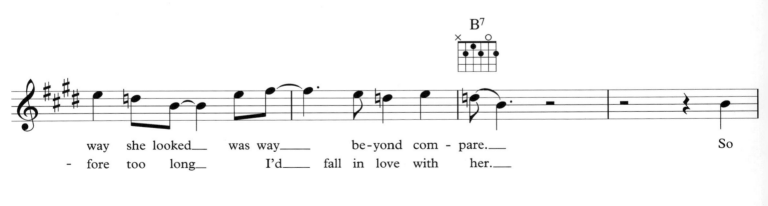

way she looked____ was way____ be-yond com - pare.____ So

- fore too long____ I'd____ fall in love with her.____

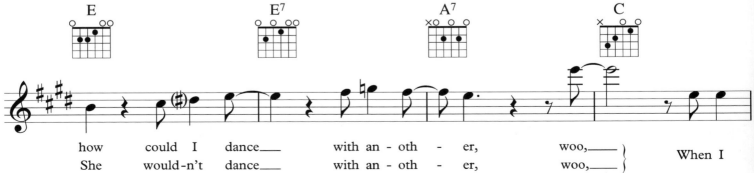

how could I dance____ with an - oth - er, woo,____ } When I

She would-n't dance____ with an - oth - er, woo,____ }

saw her stand - ing there.___   2. Well, she___   Well, my

heart   went boom___   when I   crossed   that   room,___   and   I

held   her   hand   in   mi - ne._____

_____   { Well, } we danced___   through   the   night___   and we
                   { Oh,   }

held   each   oth - er   tight,___   And   be - fore   too   long___   I___

___ fell   in   love   with   her.___   Now   I'll   nev - er   dance___

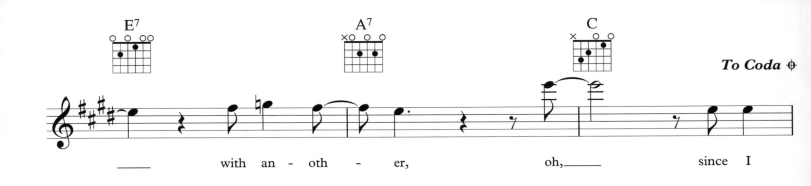

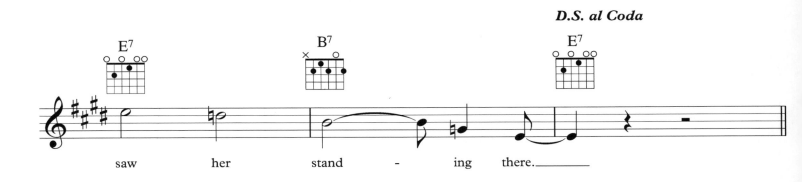

saw her stand - ing there._____

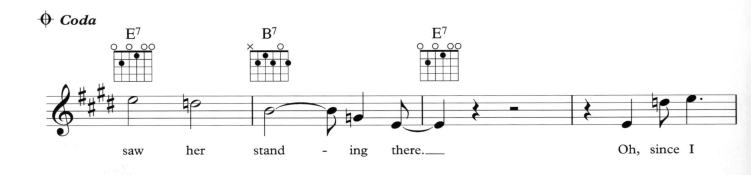

saw her stand - ing there._____ Oh, since I

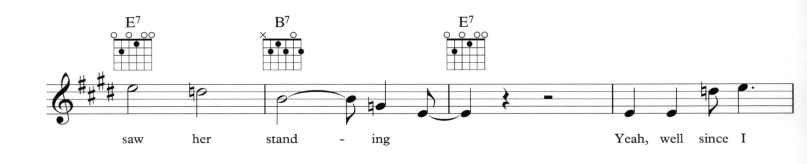

saw her stand - ing Yeah, well since I

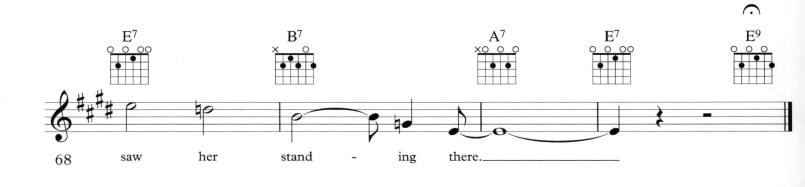

68 saw her stand - ing there._____

I Want You To Want Me

Words & Music by Rick Nielsen

Verse strumming style:

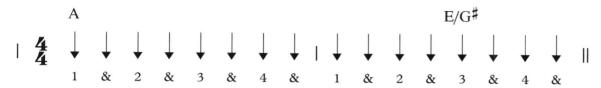

Chorus

I want you to want_ me._ I need you to need_

_ me._ I'd love you to love_ me._ I'm beg - ging you to beg_

_ me._ I want you to want_ me._ I need you to need_

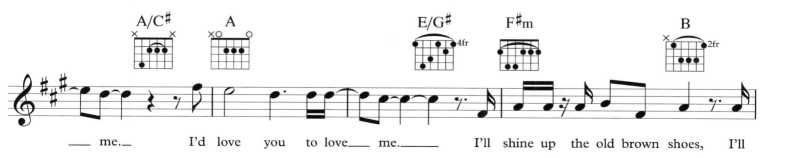

_ me._ I'd love you to love_ me._ I'll shine up the old brown shoes, I'll

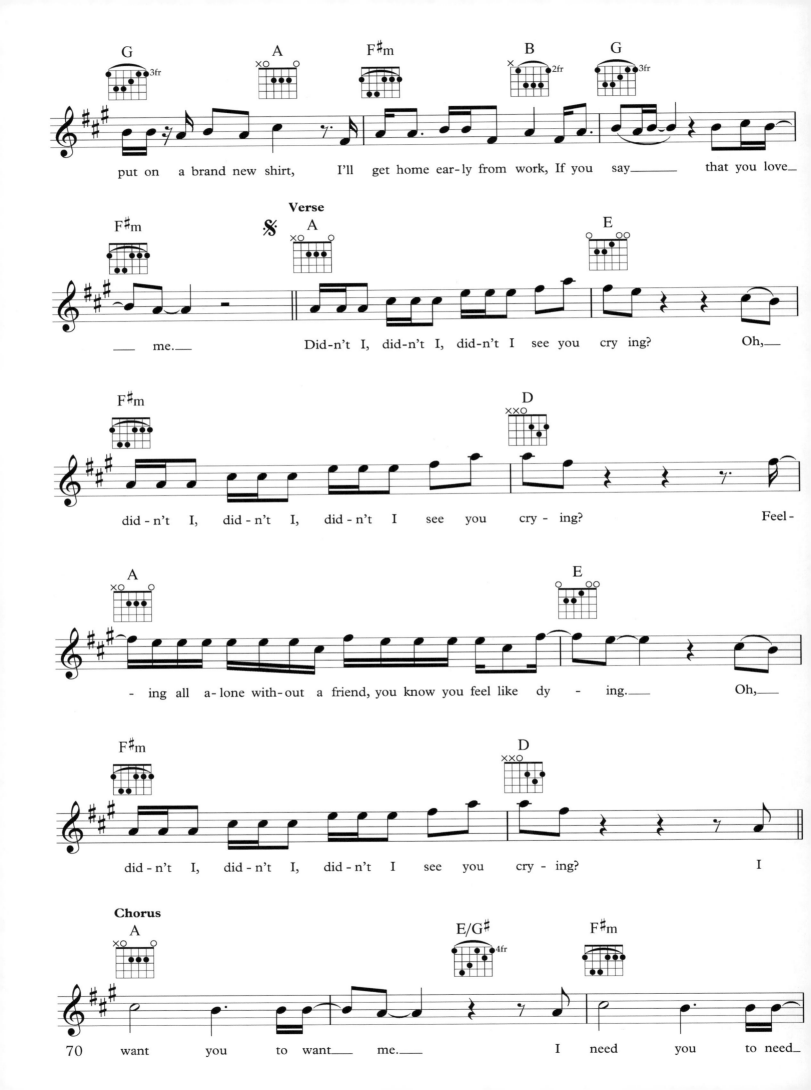

me.___ I'd love you to love___ me.___ I'm beg - ging you to beg___

___ me._____ I'll shine up the old brown shoes, I'll put on a brand new shirt, I'll

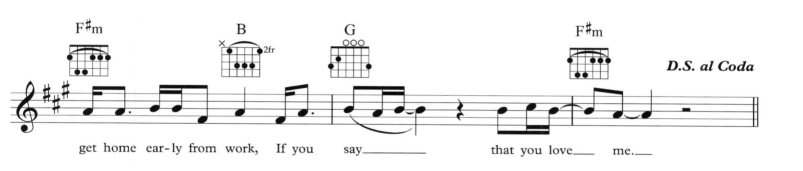

get home ear-ly from work, If you say_____ that you love___ me.___

___ me.___ I want you to want___ me.___ I

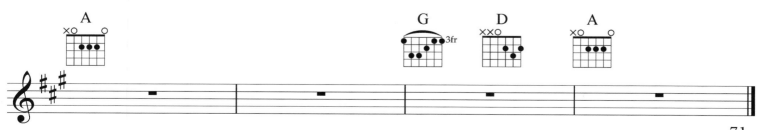

If It Makes You Happy

Words & Music by Sheryl Crow & Jeffrey Trott

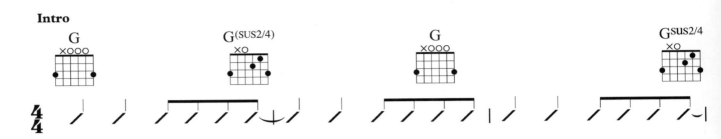

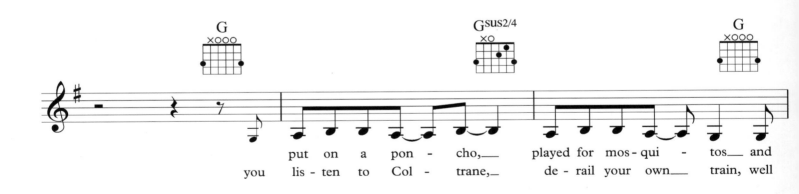

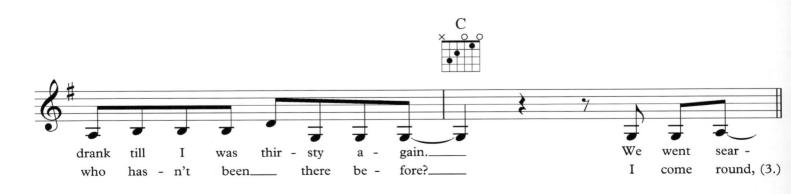

73

If it makes you hap - py,____ then why the hell__ are you__ so

1.

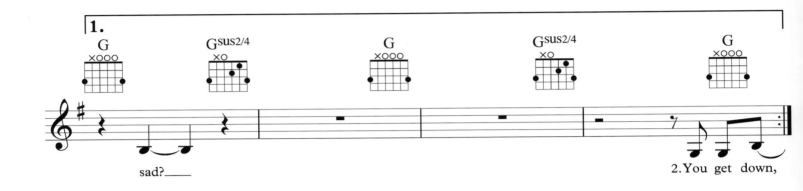

sad?____ 2.You get down,

2, 3. *To Coda* ⊕

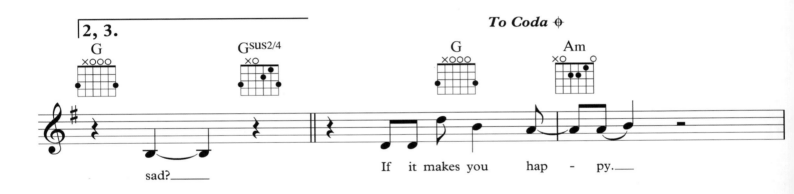

sad?____ If it makes you hap - py.____

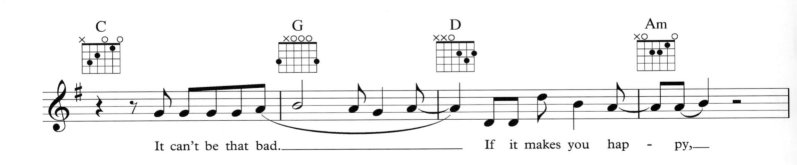

It can't be that bad.____ If it makes you hap - py,____

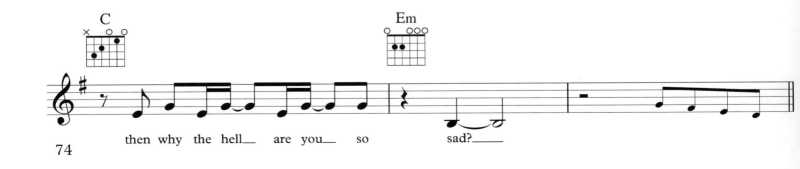

then why the hell__ are you__ so sad?____

Interlude

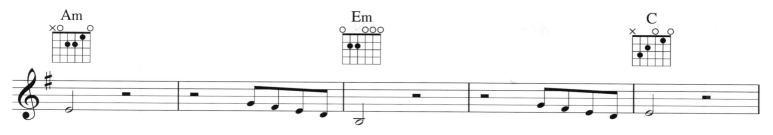

D.S. al Coda

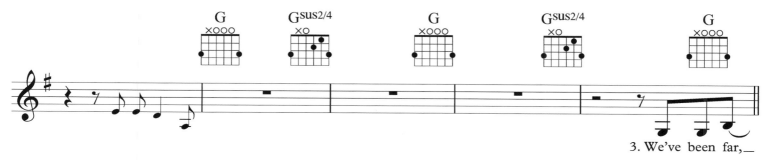

3. We've been far,__

⊕ *Coda*

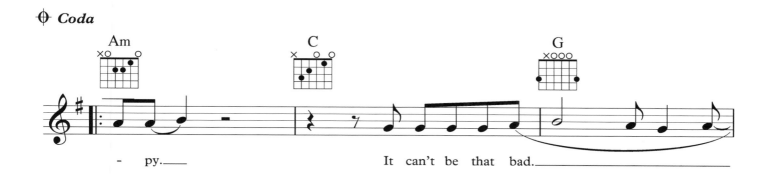

- py.___ It can't be that bad._____

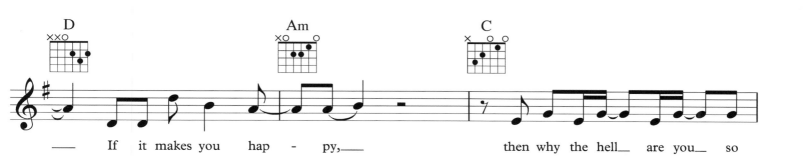

___ If it makes you hap - py,___ then why the hell__ are you__ so

Repeat to fade

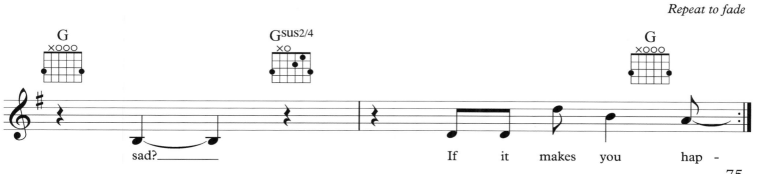

sad?_____ If it makes you hap -

Jessie's Girl

Words & Music by Rick Springfield

Bridge

And I'm look-in' in the mir - ror all the time___ won-drin' what she don't see_

___ in___ me. I've been fun-ny, I've been cool____ with the lines.___

Interlude

Ain't that the way love's sup-posed___ to___ be?

1.

2.

Tell me   where can I find   a____ wom-an like___ that?

Guitar Solo

You know I wish that I had

Outro Chorus

Jes - se's girl._____

I wish that I had

Jes - se's girl._____

I want Jes - se's girl._____

Where can I find a_____ wom-an like__ that. Like

Jes - se's girl._____

I wish that I had Jes - se's girl._____

I want I want Jes - se's girl._____

Lithium

Words & Music by Kurt Cobain

Picking style:

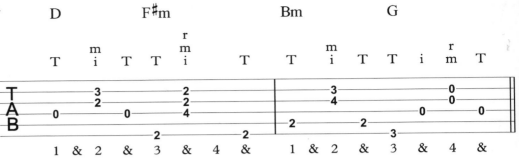

Intro

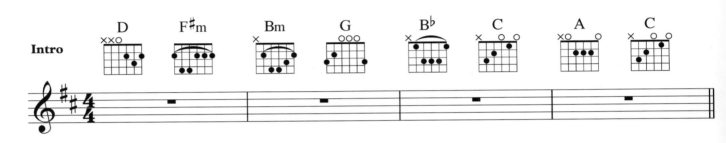

Verse

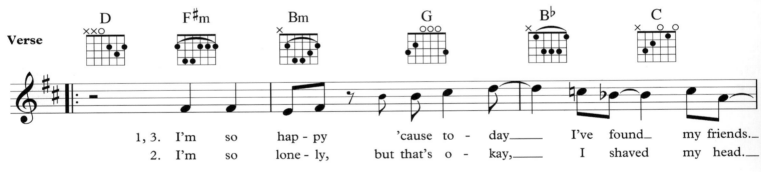

1, 3. I'm so hap-py 'cause to-day____ I've found__ my friends.

2. I'm so lone-ly, but that's o-kay,____ I shaved my head.

____ They're in my head.____ I'm so ug-ly, but that's o-kay,

__ And I'm not sad.____ And just may-be I'm to blame__

____ 'cause so____ are you.____ We broke our mir-rors. Sun-day

____ for all__ I've heard.____ But I'm not sure. I'm so ex-

mor- ning is eve-ry- day___ for all___ I care.___ And I'm not scared.___ Light my
-ci - ted, I can't wait___ to meet you there.___ But I don't care.___ I'm so

Chorus

can- dles, in a daze___ 'cause I've___found god.___ Yeah,_____
hor- ny, but that's o - kay.___ My will___ is good.___

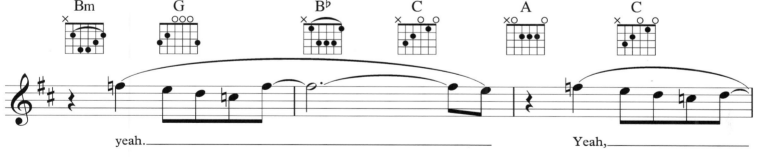

yeah._____ Yeah,_____

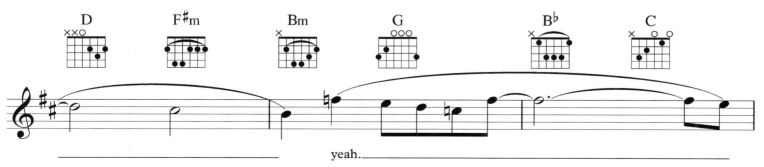

yeah._____ Yeah,_____

_____ yeah._____

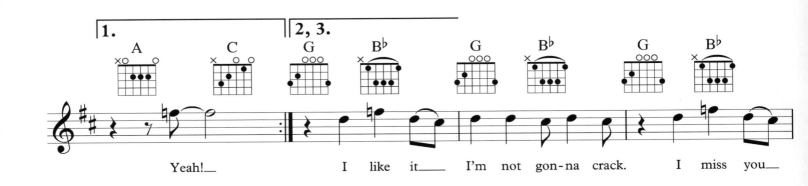

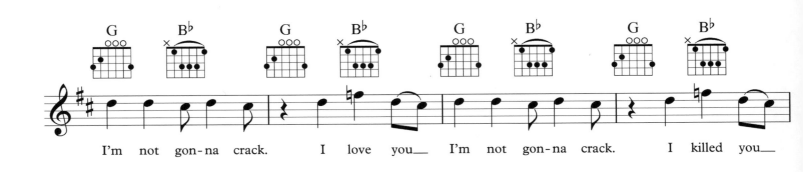

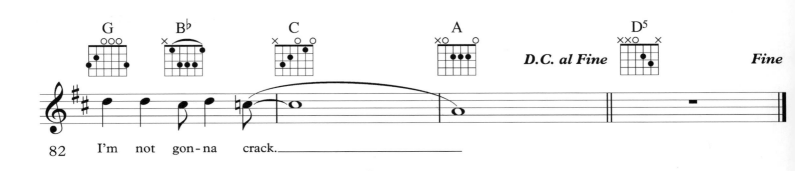

82

Livin' On A Prayer

Words & Music by Jon Bon Jovi, Richie Sambora & Desmond Child

(Guitar riff)

(Spoken:) Once upon a time, not so long ago...

Verse

1. Tom- my used to work on the docks,_____ un-ion's been on strike. He's_____
2. Tom- my's got his six- string in hock,_____ now he's_____ hold- ing in when he

down on his luck, it's tough,_____ so tough.
used to make it talk. So tough,_____ it's tough.

_____ Gi- na works the din- er all day_____
_____ Gi- na dreams of run- ning a- way;_____ when

London Calling

Words & Music by Joe Strummer, Mick Jones, Paul Simonon & Topper Headon

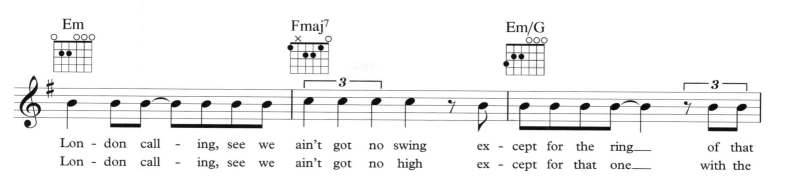

London call - ing, see we ain't got no swing ex - cept for the ring___ of that
London call - ing, see we ain't got no high ex - cept for that one___ with the

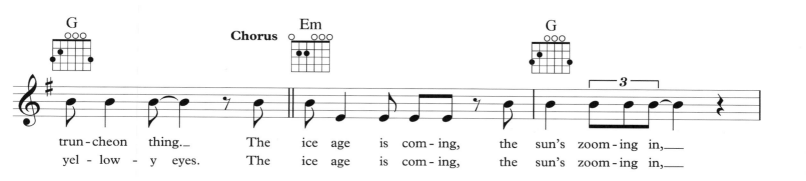

trun - cheon thing.___ The ice age is com - ing, the sun's zoom - ing in,___
yel - low - y eyes. The ice age is com - ing, the sun's zoom - ing in,___

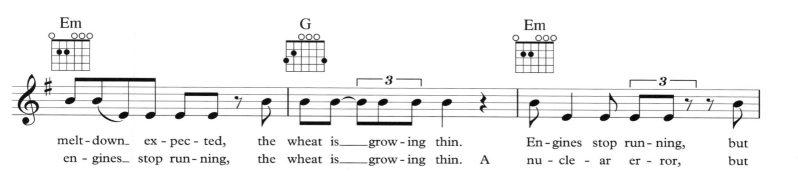

melt - down___ ex - pec - ted, the wheat is___grow - ing thin. En - gines stop run - ning, but
en - gines___ stop run - ning, the wheat is___grow - ing thin. A nu - cle - ar er - ror, but

1.

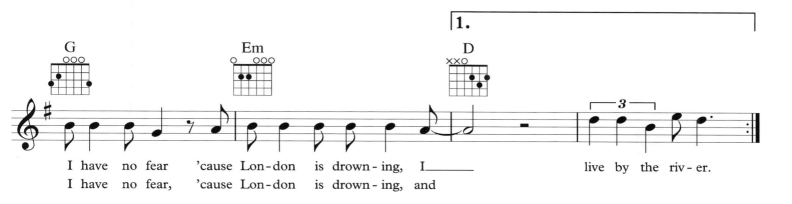

I have no fear 'cause Lon - don is drown - ing, I___ live by the riv - er.
I have no fear, 'cause Lon - don is drown - ing, and

2.

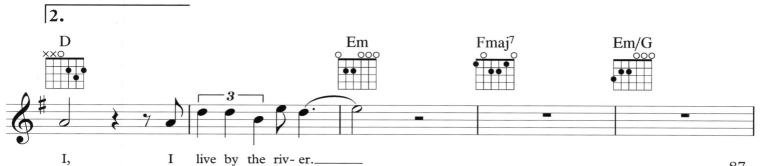

I, I live by the riv - er.___

Money For Nothing

Words & Music by Mark Knopfler & Sting

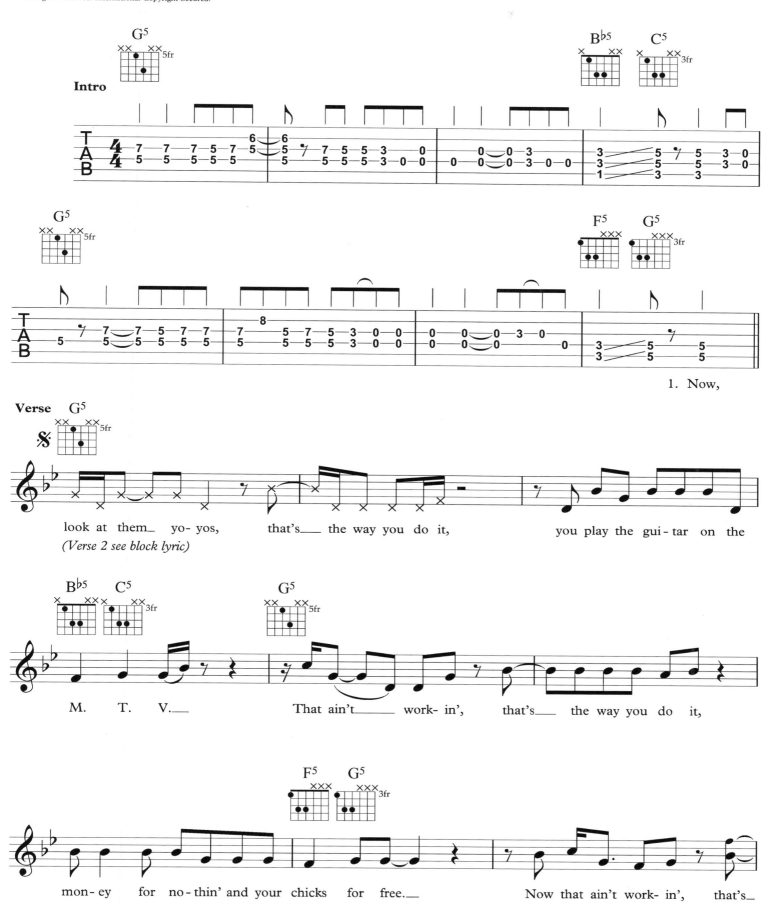

89

___ the way you do it,_ let me tell ya them_ guys ain't dumb. You

may-be get a blis-ter on your lit - tle fin - ger, may-be get a blis-ter on your_ thumb.

Chorus

We got - ta in - stall mic - ro - wave_ ov - ens, cus - tom kit - chen de -

- li - ve - ries._____ We got - ta move these re - fri - ge - ra - tors,

we got - ta move these co - lour T. V.s_____ Ow!

Interlude

(as Intro)

To Coda ⊕

90

Play Chorus

⊕ *Coda*

that ain't work- in'   that's the way you do it,   you play the gui- tar on the M. T. V.

That ain't work- in',   that's___ the way you do it,   mon- ey for no- thin' and your chicks   for free.

Outro

Mo- ney   for no- thin'   and your chicks for free._   Get your

Repeat to fade

mon- ey   for no -thin'   and your chicks for free._

Verse 2:
I should have learned to play the guitar,
I should have learned to play them drums,
Look at that mama, she got it stickin' in the camera.
Man, we could have some fun.
And he's up there, what's that? Hawaiian noises?
He's bangin' on the bongos like a chimpanzee,
Oh that ain't workin', that's the way you do it,
Get your money for nothin', get your chicks for free.

More Than A Feeling

Words & Music by Tom Scholz

Verse

1. I looked out this mor - ning and the sun was gone,_ turned on some mu - sic to
(Verse 2 see block lyrics)

start my_ day._ I lost my - self_ in a fa - mil - iar song, I

closed my_ eyes_ and I slipped a - way._

(Guitar)

It's

3. When I'm tired and think- -ing cold I hide in my mu - sic, for-get the day, and dream of a girl I used to know. I closed my eyes and she slipped a - way.

She slipped a - way

94

Verse 2:
So many people have come and gone,
Their faces fade as the years go by,
Yet I still recall as I wander on,
As clear as the sun in the summer sky.

95

Paperback Writer

Words & Music by John Lennon & Paul McCartney

Intro riff:

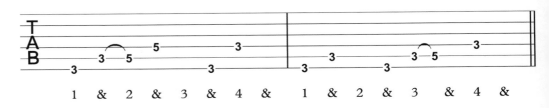

1 & 2 & 3 & 4 & 1 & 2 & 3 & 4 &

Intro

N.C.

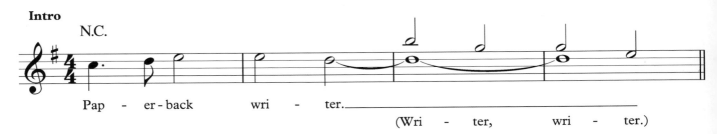

Pap - er-back wri - ter._____ (Wri - ter, wri - ter.)

G⁷

(Guitar) 1.Dear_

Verse G⁷

Sir or Mad - am, will you read my book, it took me years to write. Will you take a look? It's
(Verses 2, 3 & 4 see block lyrics)

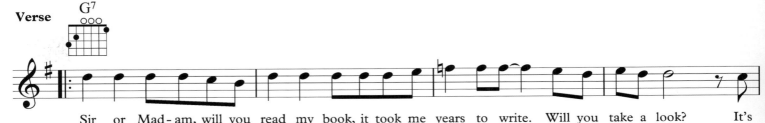

based on a nov-el by a man named Lear and I need a job,__ so I want to be a pa-per-back

1. **2.**

C G⁷ G⁷

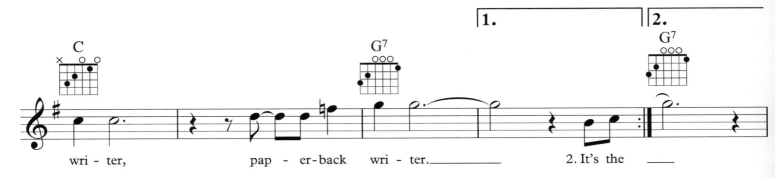

wri - ter, pap - er-back wri - ter._____ 2. It's the ___

Pap - er-back wri - ter._____ *(Guitar)*
(Pap - er-back wri - ter, wri - ter.)

3.

3. It's a ___ If you

4.

___ Pap - er-back wri - ter._____ *(Guitar)*
(Pap - er-back wri - ter, wri - ter.)

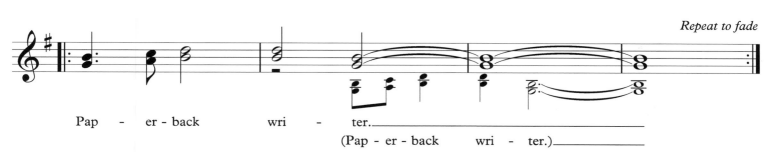

Repeat to fade

Pap - er - back wri - ter._____
(Pap - er - back wri - ter.)_____

Verse 2:
It's the dirty story of a dirty man,
And his clinging wife doesn't understand.
His son is working for the Daily Mail,
It's a steady job,
But he wants to be a paperback writer,
Paperback writer.

Verse 3:
It's a thousand pages give or take a few,
I'll be writing more in a week or two.
I can make it longer if you like the style,
I can change it 'round,
And I want to be a paperback writer,
Paperback writer.

Verse 4:
If you really like it you can have the rights,
It could make a million for you overnight.
If you must return it you can send it here,
But I need a break,
And I want to be a paperback writer,
Paperback writer.

Mr. Brightside

Written by Brandon Flowers & Dave Keuning

Capo: Fret 1

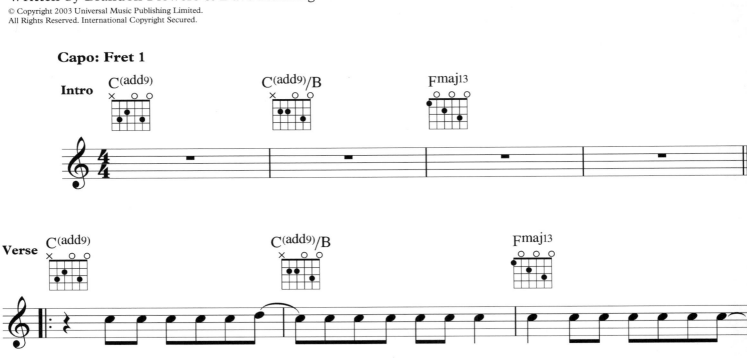

Intro C(add9)   C(add9)/B   Fmaj13

Verse C(add9)   C(add9)/B   Fmaj13

Com-ing out of my cage,___ and I've been do-ing just fine. Got-ta, got-ta be down___

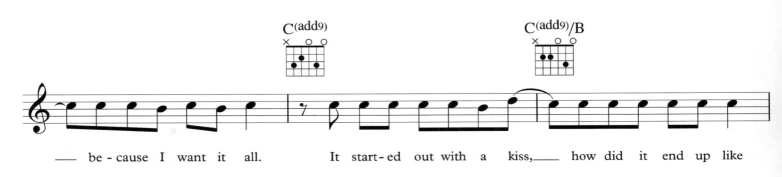

C(add9)   C(add9)/B

___ be-cause I want it all. It start-ed out with a kiss,___ how did it end up like

Fmaj13   C(add9)

this? It was on-ly a kiss,___ it was on-ly a kiss. Now I'm fall-ing a-sleep___

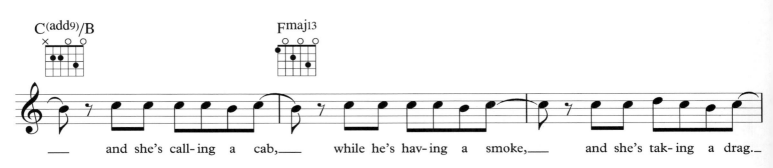

C(add9)/B   Fmaj13

___ and she's call-ing a cab,___ while he's hav-ing a smoke,___ and she's tak-ing a drag.

Now they're go-ing to bed___ and my sto-mach is sick,___ and it's all in his head___

Bridge

___ but she's touch-ing his chest now. He takes off her dress now,

let-ting me go.___

And I just can't look; it's kill-ing me and

tak-ing___ con-trol.

Chorus

Jea-lou-sy turn-ing saints in to the sea, turn-ing through sick

99

The Passenger

Words by James Osterberg
Music by James Osterberg & Ricky Gardiner

Strumming style:

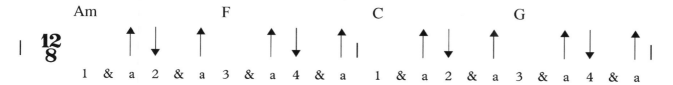

Intro

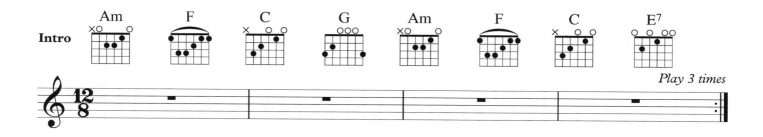

Play 3 times

Verse

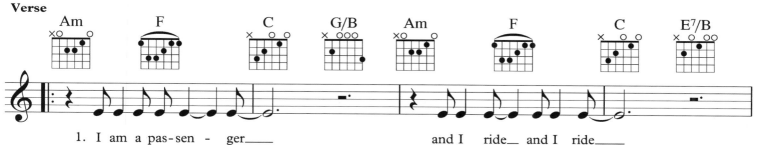

1. I am a pas-sen - ger____   and I ride__ and I ride____
2. I am a pas-sen - ger____   I stay un - der - glass____
3. Get in - to the__ car,____   we'll be the pas-sen - ger,____

(Verses 4 & 5 see block lyrics)

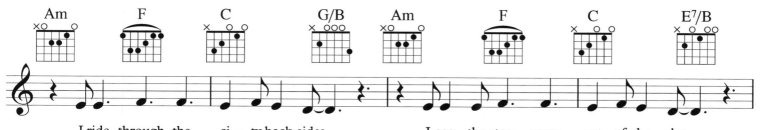

I ride through the   ci - ty back-sides__   I see the stars come   out of the sky,__
I look through my   win-dow so bright__   I see the stars come   out____ to - night,__
we'll ride through the   ci - ty to - night,__   see the ci-ty's__   ripped back-sides.__

stars made for us to - night.___

I sing, la, la, la, la, la, la, la, la,___

la, la, la, la, la, la, la, la,___

Verse 4
Oh, the passenger,
How, how he rides.
Oh, the passenger,
He rides and he rides.
He looks through his window,
What does he see?
He sees the sight of hollow sky,
He sees the stars come out tonight,
He sees the city's ripped backsides,
He sees the winding ocean drive.
And everything was made for you and me,
All of it was made for you and me,
But it just belongs to you and me.
So let's take a ride and see what's mine.

I say, la, la, la, la, la, la, la, la,
La, la, la, la, la, la, la, la,
La, la, la, la, la, la, la, la, la, la, la.

Verse 5
Oh, the passenger,
He rides and he rides,
He sees things from under glass,
He looks through his window side,
He sees the things he knows are his,
He sees the bright and hollow sky,
He sees the city sleep at night,
He sees the skies are out tonight.
And all of it is yours and mine,
And all of it is yours and mine,
So let's ride and ride and ride and ride.

I say, la, la, la, la, la, la, la, la,
La, la, la, la, la, la, la, la,
La, la, la, la, la, la, la, la, la, la, la, etc.

Rock And Roll All Nite

Words & Music by Paul Stanley & Gene Simmons

The chords shown in this song have a 'pushed' or anticipated feel—meaning that they're generally played a half-beat before the beginning of the bar.

To match recording tune guitar one semitone down

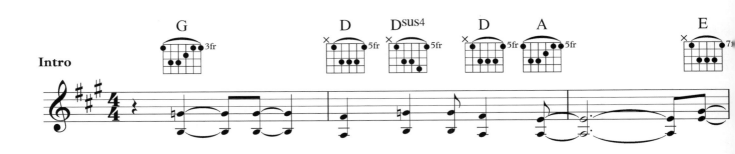

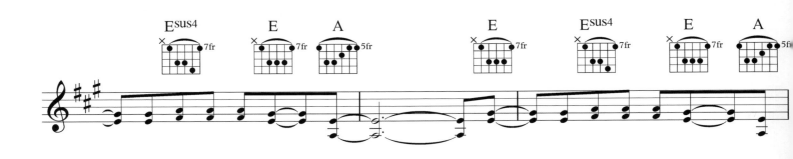

1. You   show us   eve-ry-thing you've got.___   You keep on dan-cin' and the
3. You keep on sa-ying you'll be   mine for a   while.   You're loo-kin' fan-cy and I

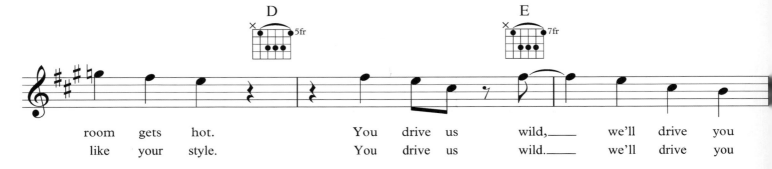

room   gets   hot.   You drive us   wild,___   we'll   drive   you
like   your   style.   You drive us   wild.___   we'll   drive   you

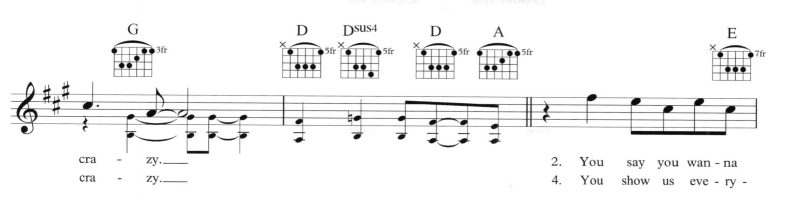

cra - zy.____
cra - zy.____

2. You say you wan - na
4. You show us eve - ry -

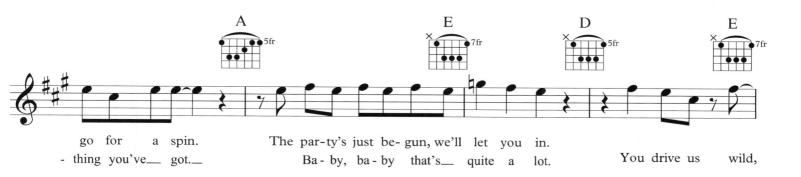

go for a spin.   The par - ty's just be - gun, we'll let you in.
- thing you've__ got.__   Ba - by, ba - by that's__ quite a lot.   You drive us wild,

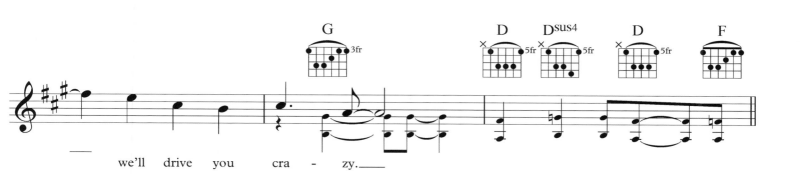

____   we'll drive you cra - zy.____

Pre-Chorus

You keep on shou - tin', you____ keep on shou - tin'...   I__

Chorus

_____   wan - na rock and_ roll__ all__ night_____   and par - ty e - ve - ry day.

I_____ wan-na rock and roll__ all__ night_____ and par-ty e-ve-ry day.

I_____ wan-na rock and_ roll__ all__ night_____ and par-ty e-ve-ry day.

I____ wan-na rock and_ roll__ all__ night_____ and par-ty e-ve-ry day.

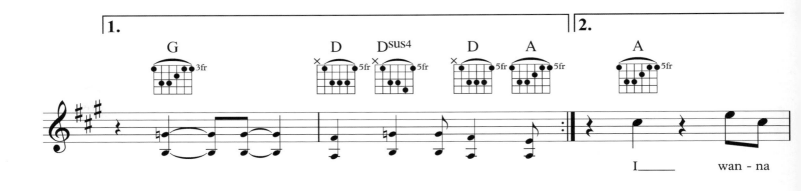

I_____ wan - na

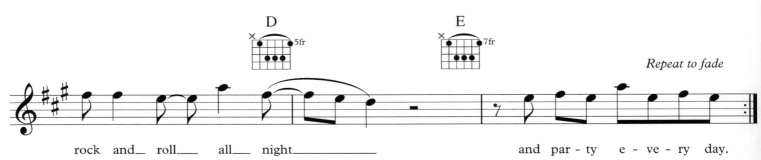

Repeat to fade

rock and_ roll____ all__ night_____ and par-ty e-ve-ry day.

Roxanne

Words & Music by Sting

1. Rox - anne, you ___ don't have to ___
(2.) loved you since I knew ya, I

___ put on the red light, ___ those days are ov -
would-n't talk down to ya, ___ I have to tell you just how I

- er, you don't have to ___ sell your bo - dy to the night. ___ Rox -
feel, I won't share ___ you with an - oth - er boy. ___ I

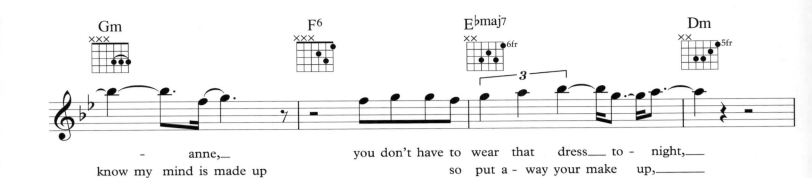

- anne,— you don't have to wear that dress— to - night,—
know my mind is made up so put a - way your make up,———

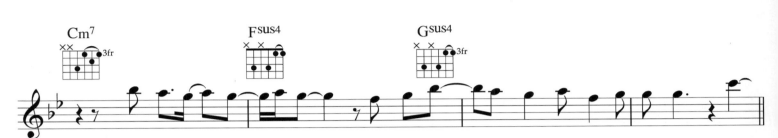

walk the streets_ for——mo-ney,— you don't care—— if it's wrong or if it's right. Rox-
told you once I won't_ tell you a-gain it's a crime—— the way...

Pre-Chorus

- anne,—— you don't have to put on the red—— light.—— Rox -

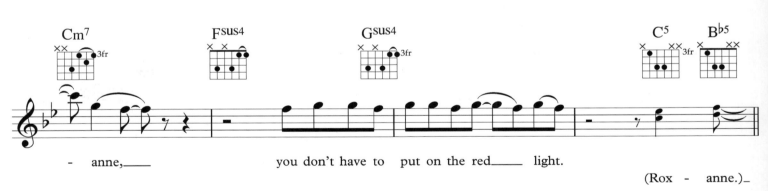

- anne,—— you don't have to put on the red—— light.

(Rox - anne.)_

Chorus

Put on the red_ light. Put on the red——— light.

_____ (Rox - anne.)_____ (Rox - anne.)_

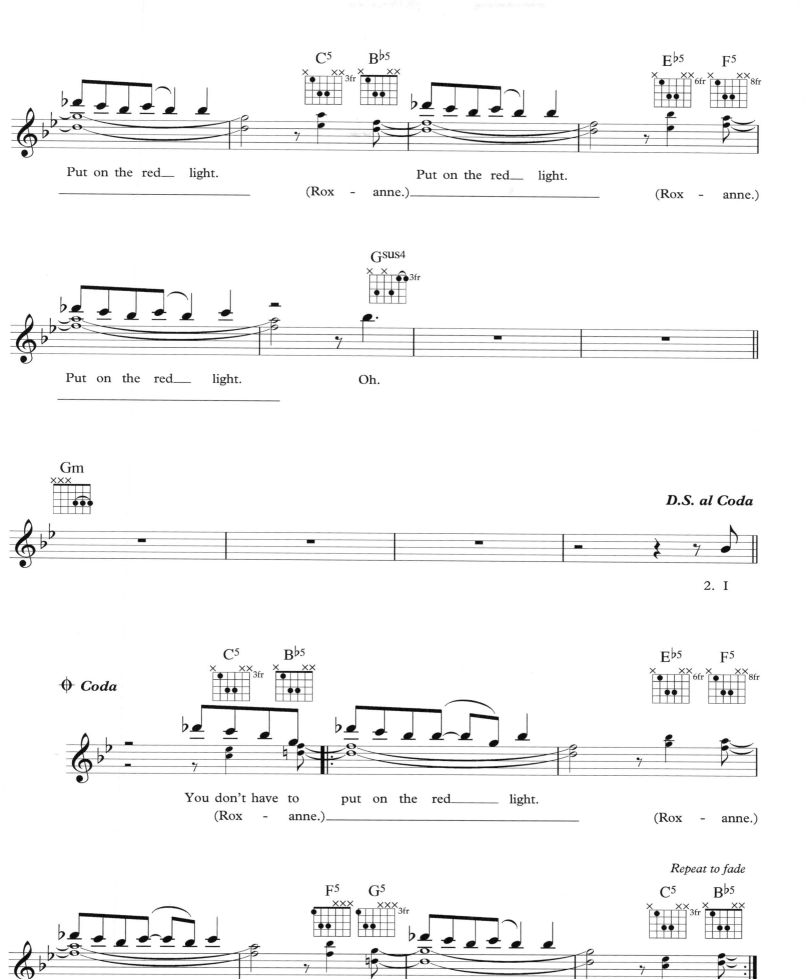

Put on the red___ light.

(Rox - anne.)

Put on the red___ light.

(Rox - anne.)

Put on the red___ light.

Oh.

Gm

D.S. al Coda

2. I

✛ *Coda*

You don't have to put on the red_____ light.

(Rox - anne.)

(Rox - anne.)

Repeat to fade

Put on the red_____ light.

Put on the red___ light.

(Rox - anne.)

(Rox - anne.___

Sex On Fire

Words & Music by Caleb Followill, Nathan Followill, Jared Followill & Matthew Followill

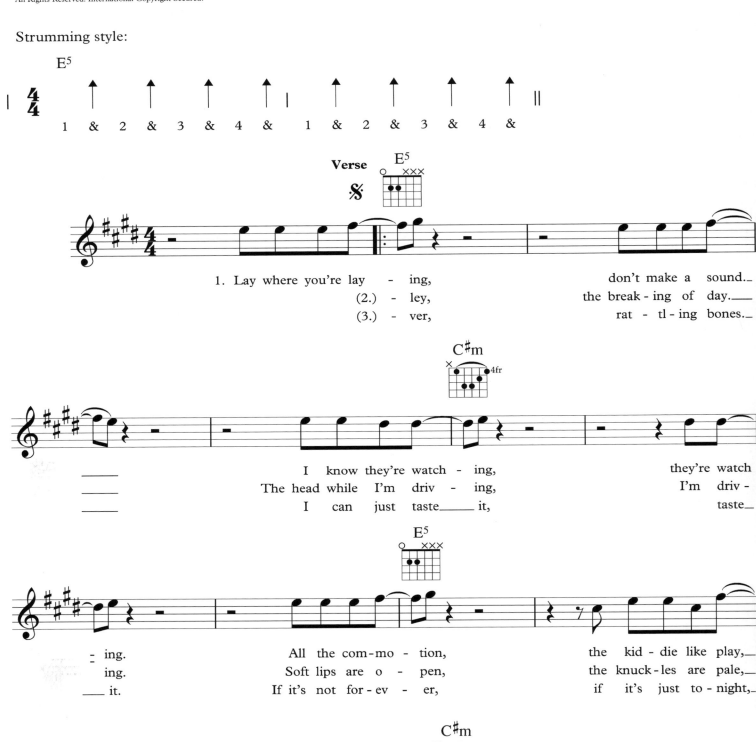

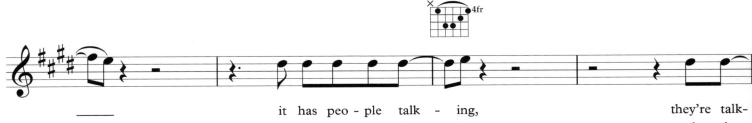

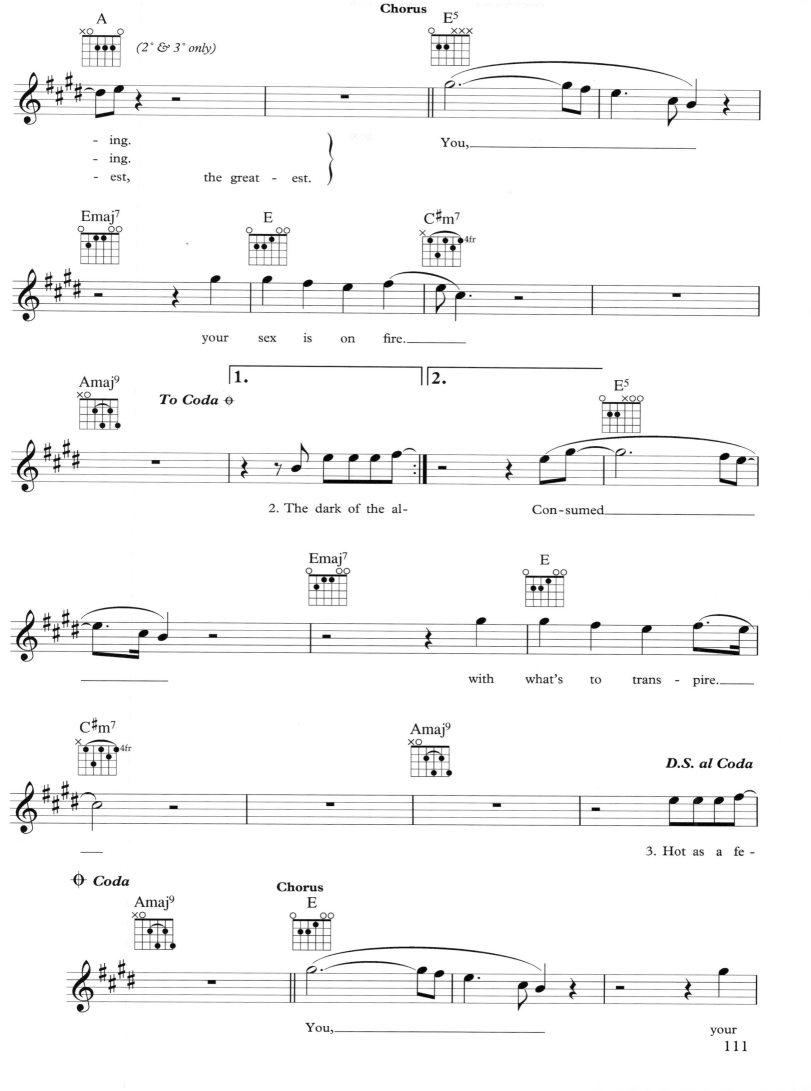

Should I Stay Or Should I Go

Words & Music by Mick Jones & Joe Strummer

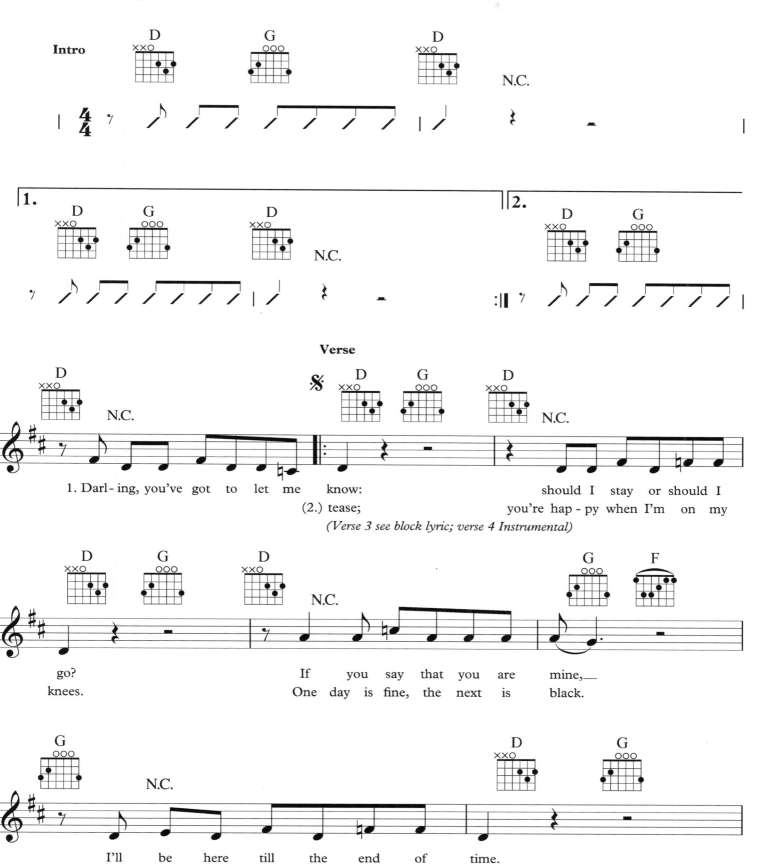

So you've got to let me know:—
well, come on and let me know:—
should I stay or should I

1, 3.
go?
2. It's al - ways tease, tease,
4. *Instrumental*
should I stay or should I

2, 4.
should I stay or should I

go now?
(Chorus 2 see block lyrics)
Should I stay or should I go now?

If I go there will be trou - ble,——— and if I stay it will be

To Coda ⊕
dou - ble.
So come on and let me know:————
So you got - ta let me

D.S. al Coda
3. This in - de - ci - sion's bug - ging

Coda

know:_____ should I cool it or should I blow?

Should I stay or should I go now? If I go there will be trou ble,_____

and if I stay it will be dou - ble. So you got - ta let me

know:_____ Should I stay or should I go?

Verse 3
This indecision's bugging me
(Esta indecision me molesta)
If you don't want me, set me free
(Si no me quieres, librame)
Exactly who'm I supposed to be
(Digame que teno ser)
Don't you know which clothes even fit me?
(¿No sabes que ropas me queda?)
Come on and let me know
(Me tienes que desir)
Should I cool it or should I blow?
(¿Me debo ir o quedarme?)

Chorus 2
Should I stay or should I go now?
(¿Yo me frio o lo soplo?)
Should I stay or should I go now?
(¿Yo me frio o lo soplo?)
If I go there will be trouble
(Si me voy a ver peligro)
And if I stay it will be double
(Si me quedo sera el doble)
So you gotta let me know
(Me tienes que decir)...

Since You've Been Gone

Words & Music by Russ Ballard

This version is from Rainbow's 1979 album *Down To Earth*. However, to play along with their single version of this song, you'll need to put a capo on the 1st fret.

1. I get the same old dreams, same time ev'ry night,
2. So in the night I stand, be-neath the back-street light,

fall to the ground an' I wake up,
I read the words that you sent to me.

so I get out of bed put on my shoes an' in my head
I can take the af-ter-noon but night-time comes a-round too soon,

C   **G/B**   **A(add9)**   **D(add9)**   **E♭5**

thoughts_ fly back____ to the break   up,   these____ four walls are clo -
you____ can't know what you mean to me.____   Your poi - son let - ter, your

F5   **E♭5**   **A5**   **D5**

- sin' in.   Look at the fix you've____ put____ me__ in.____
te - le - gram,   just goes to show you don't give____ a____ damn.____

Chorus

G5   **D5**   **E5**   **C5**   **G5**   **D5**   **E5**

Since you've been gone,   since you've been gone   I'm out of my head, can't   take_

C5   **D5**   **G5**   **D5**   **E5**   **C5**

___ it.   Could I be wrong,   but since you've been gone____

G5   **D5**   **E5**   **C5**   **D5**   **G5**   **D5**

you cast a spell,_ so___ break___ it.   Oh_____

E5   **C5**   **G5**   **D5**   **E5**   **C5**   **D5**

oh_____   oh_____   since you've been gone.

117

you cast a spell_ so___ break___ it._ Oh_____

oh_____ oh_____ oh_____

ev - er since you've been gone._____

Guitar Solo

Outro Chorus

Since you've been gone,___ since you've been gone,___ I'm

Fade

out of my head, can't take___ it.

Song 2

Music by Damon Albarn, Graham Coxon, Alex James & David Rowntree

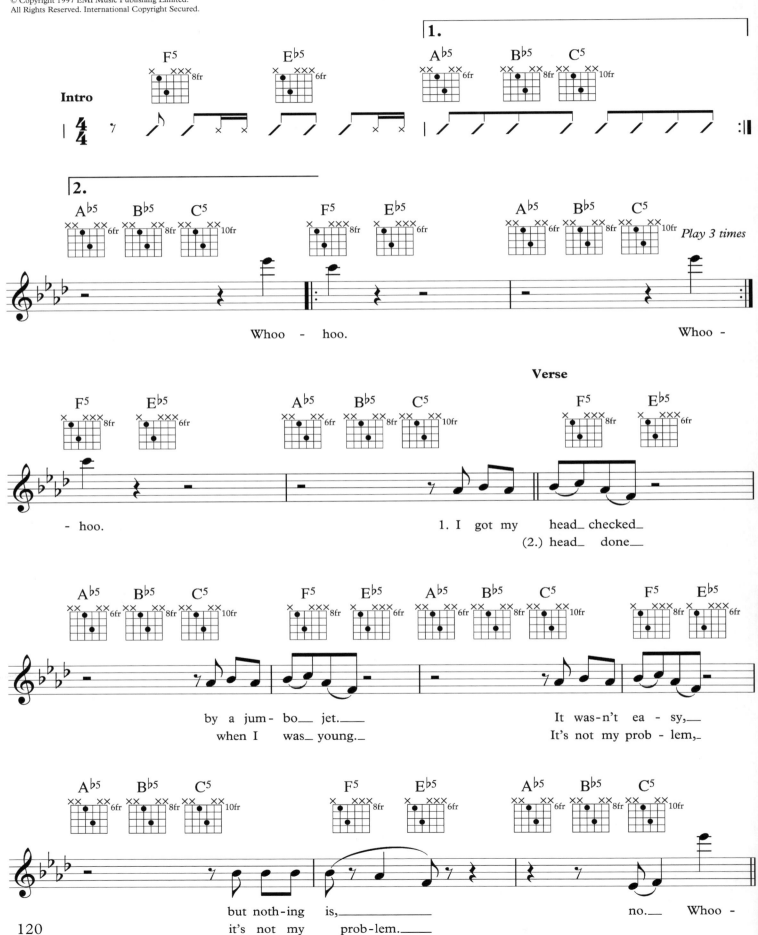

Smells Like Teen Spirit

Words & Music by Kurt Cobain, Dave Grohl & Krist Novoselic

Substitute

Words & Music by Pete Townshend

Intro riff:

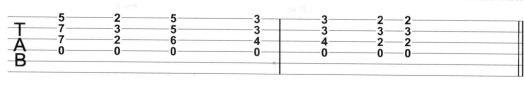

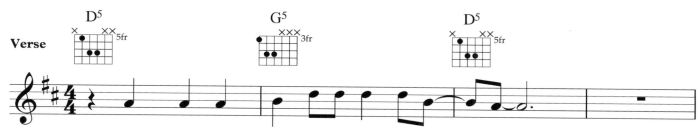

Verse

1. You think we look pret-ty good to-geth - er.___
2. *(D.C.)* I was born with a plas - tic spoon in my mouth.

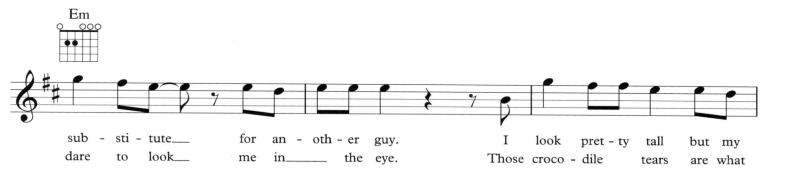

You think my shoes are made of leath - er.___ But I'm a
The north side in my town faced east and the east was fac - ing south.. And now you

sub - sti - tute___ for an - oth - er guy. I look pret - ty tall but my
dare to look___ me in___ the eye. Those croco - dile tears are what

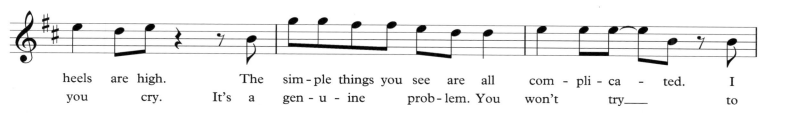

heels are high. The sim - ple things you see are all com - pli - ca - ted. I
you cry. It's a gen - u - ine prob - lem. You won't try___ to

look pret - ty young but I'm just back - dat - ed, yeah._____
work it out at all, just pass it by, pass it by._____

Chorus

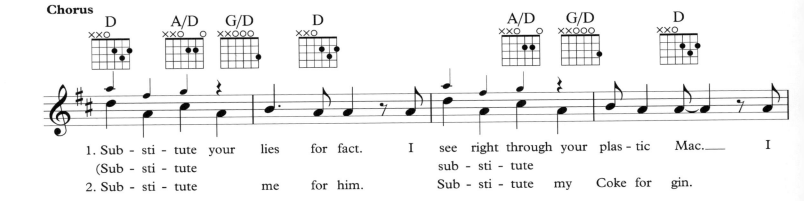

1. Sub - sti - tute your lies for fact. I see right through your plas - tic Mac.___ I
   (Sub - sti - tute   sub - sti - tute
2. Sub - sti - tute me for him. Sub - sti - tute my Coke for gin.

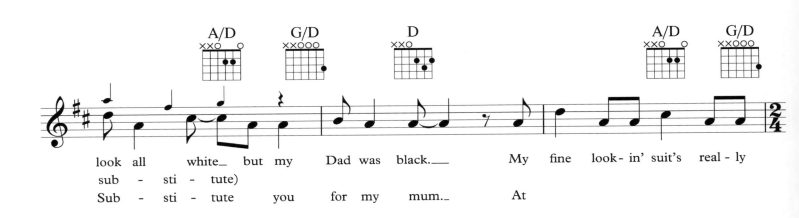

look all white___ but my Dad was black.___ My fine look - in' suit's real - ly
sub - sti - tute)
Sub - sti - tute you for my mum.___ At

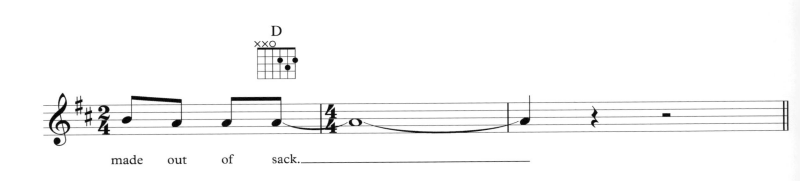

made out of sack._____

Instrumental

N.C.

1.

Sultans Of Swing

Words & Music by Mark Knopfler

Strumming style:

Intro

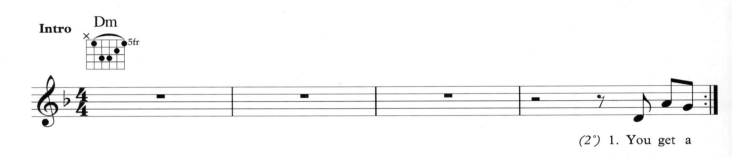

(2°) 1. You get a

Verse

shiv-er in the dark, it's a rain-ing in the park, but mean - time,
(2.) step in - side__ but you don't see too ma - ny fa - ces,
(Verses 3-5 & 7 see block lyrics)
(Verse 6 instrumental)

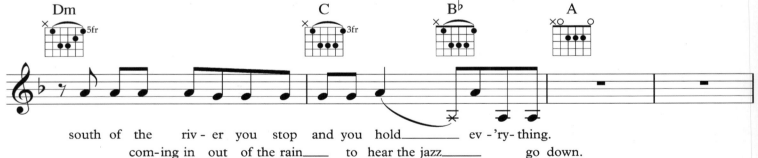

south of the riv-er you stop and you hold_____ ev-'ry-thing.
com-ing in out of the rain___ to hear the jazz_____ go down.

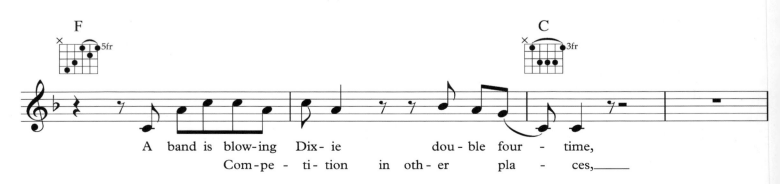

A band is blow-ing Dix - ie dou - ble four - time,
Com-pe - ti-tion in oth - er pla - ces,

Guitar Solo

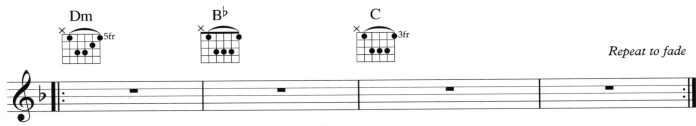

Repeat to fade

Verse 3
You check out Guitar George, he knows all the chords,
Mind he's strictly rhythm, he doesn't want to make it to cry or sing.
Yes, and an old guitar is all he can afford
When he gets up under the lights to play his thing.

Verse 4
And Harry doesn't mind if he doesn't make the scene,
He's got a daytime job, he's doing alright.
He can play the honky-tonk like anything,
Saving it up Friday night,
With the Sultans, with the Sultans of Swing.

Verse 5
And a crowd of young boys, they're fooling around in the corner,
Drunk and dressed in their best brown baggies and their platform soles.
They don't give a damn about any trumpet-playing band,
It ain't what they call rock and roll.
And the Sultans, yeah the Sultans they play Creole.

Verse 6 (Instrumental)

Verse 7
And then the man he steps right up to the microphone,
And says at last just as the time bell rings.
'Goodnight, now it's time to go home.'
And he makes it fast with one more thing,
'We are the Sultans, we are the Sultans of Swing.'

Summer Of '69

Words & Music by Bryan Adams & Jim Vallance

© Copyright 1984 Almo Music Corporation/Adams Communications Inc/Testatyme Music/Irving Music.
Rondor Music (London) Limited.

Strumming style:

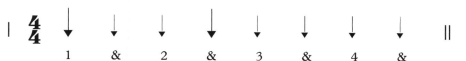

Play detached, constant down-strums, accenting the first and fourth strum in each bar.

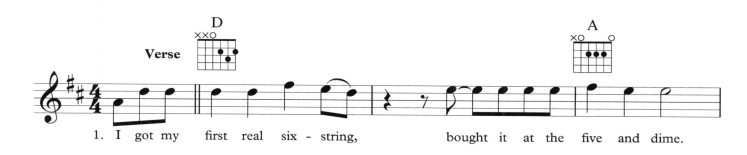

Verse

1. I got my first real six - string, bought it at the five and dime.

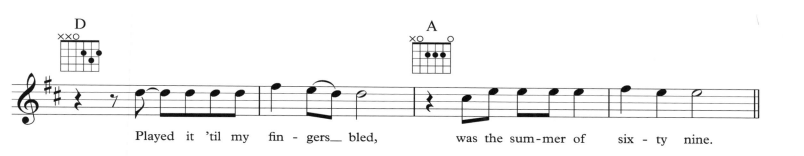

Played it 'til my fin - gers_ bled, was the sum-mer of six - ty nine.

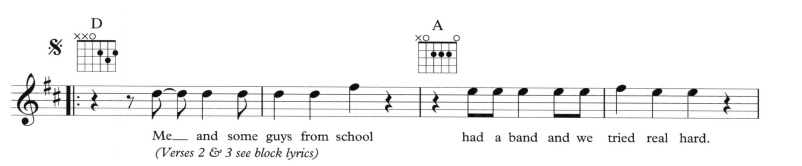

Me_ and some guys from school had a band and we tried real hard.
(Verses 2 & 3 see block lyrics)

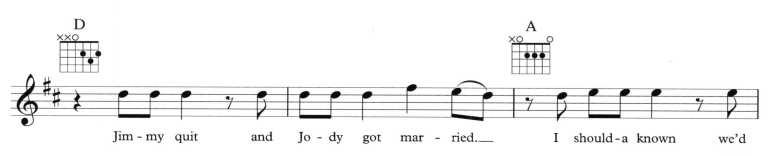

Jim - my quit and Jo - dy got mar - ried._ I should-a known we'd

Bridge

Man,— we were kill - in' time,— we were young and rest - less, we

need-ed to— un-wind. I guess noth-in' can last— for - ev - er, for - ev-

- er,——— no!

D.S. al Coda

Coda

Repeat ad lib. to fade

six - ty nine.—— Back in the sum-mer of

Verse 2:
Ain't no use complainin' when you got a job to do,
Spent my evenin's down at the drive-in, and that's when I met you.

Bridge:
Standin' on your mama's porch, you told me that you'd wait forever,
Oh, and when you held my hand, I knew that it was now or never.
Those were the best days of my life.

Verse 3:
And now the times are changin', look at everything that's come and gone,
Sometimes when I play that old six-string I think about you, wonder what went wrong.

Bridge:
Standin' on your mama's porch, you told me it'd last forever,
Oh, and when you held my hand, I knew that it was now or never.
Those were the best days of my life.

133

Teenage Kicks

Words & Music by John O'Neill

Strumming style:

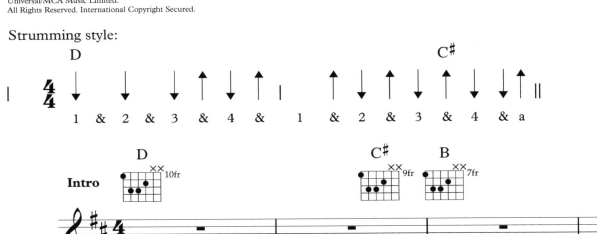

Intro

Verse

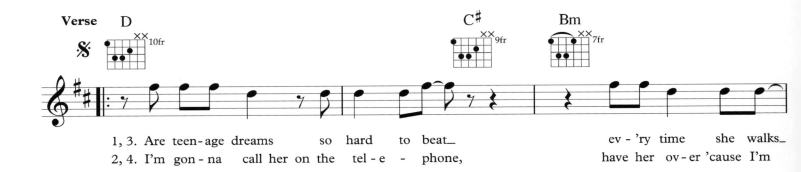

1, 3. Are teen-age dreams so hard to beat_ ev-'ry time she walks_

2, 4. I'm gon-na call her on the tel-e-phone, have her ov-er 'cause I'm

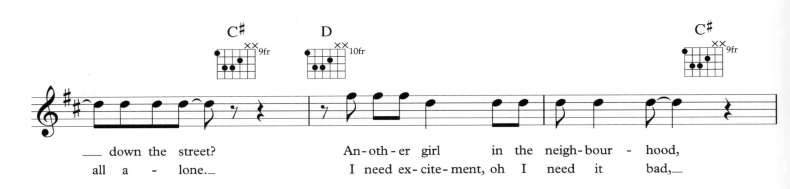

_ down the street?

all a-lone._

An-oth-er girl in the neigh-bour-hood,

I need ex-cite-ment, oh I need it bad,_

Chorus

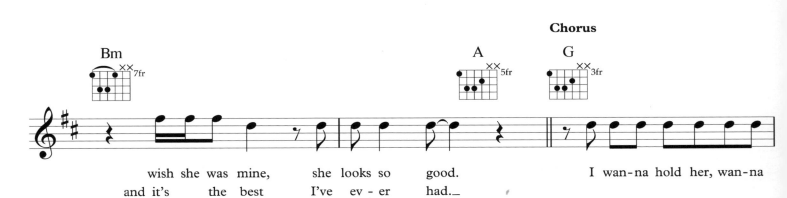

wish she was mine, she looks so good.

and it's the best I've ev-er had._

I wan-na hold her, wan-na

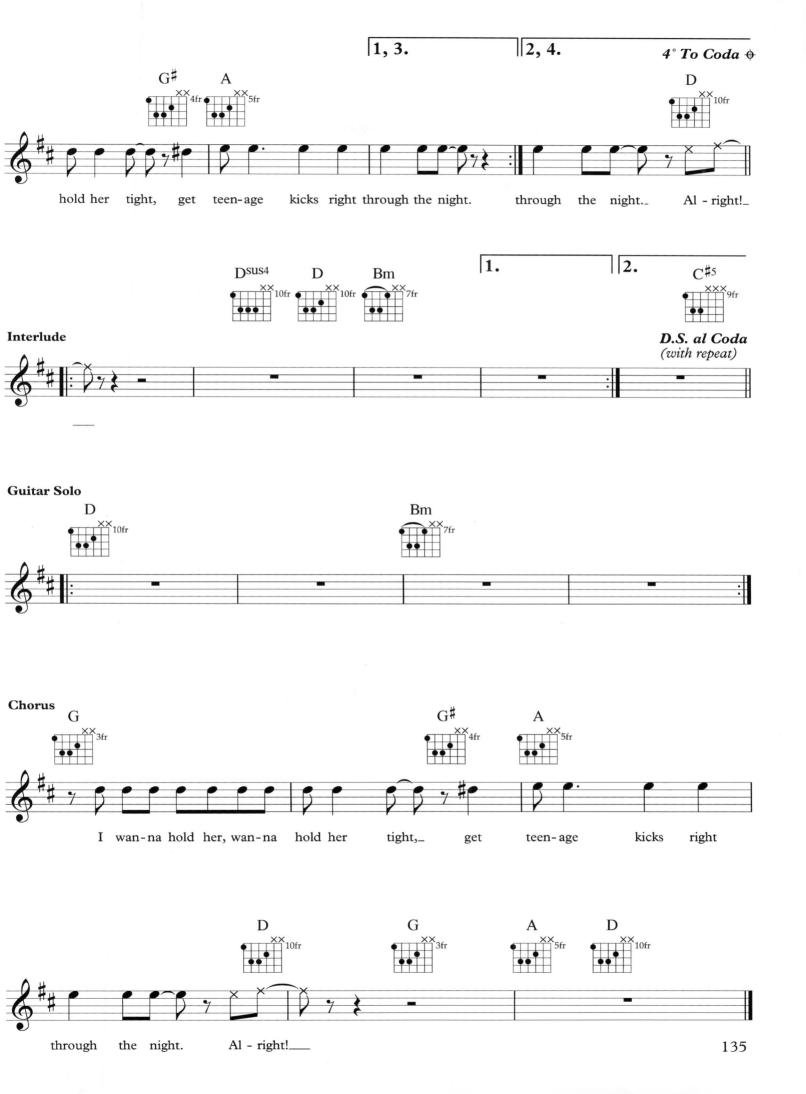

Supersonic

Words & Music by Noel Gallagher

Intro riff:

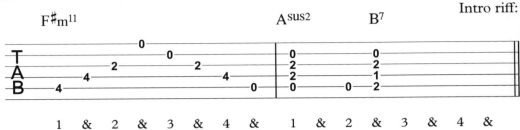

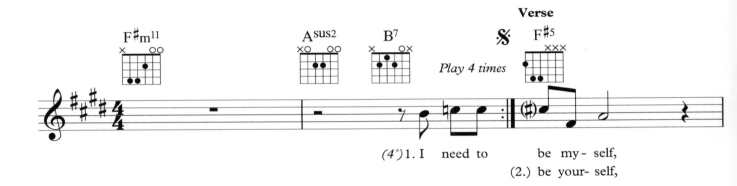

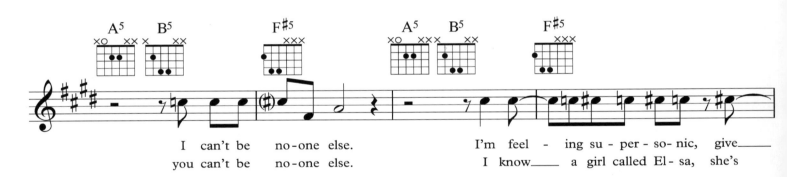

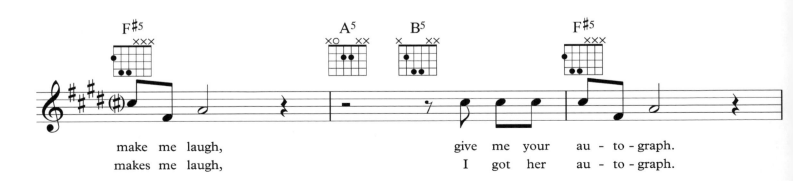

Can I ride____ with you____ in your B.____ M. W.?_____ You can
She done it with a doc-tor on____ a he-li-cop-ter, she's

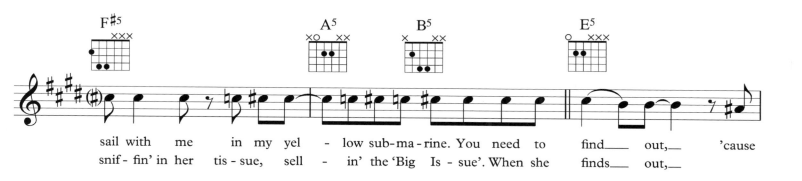

sail with me in my yel - low sub-ma-rine. You need to find____ out,____ 'cause
snif-fin' in her tis-sue, sell - in' the 'Big Is-sue'. When she finds____ out,____

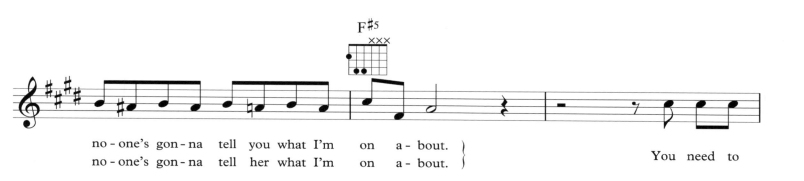

no-one's gon-na tell you what I'm on a - bout.
no-one's gon-na tell her what I'm on a - bout.

You need to

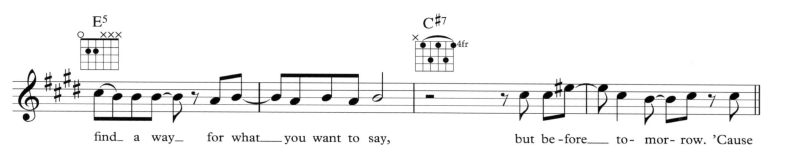

find_ a way_ for what____you want to say, but be-fore____ to-mor - row. 'Cause

Chorus

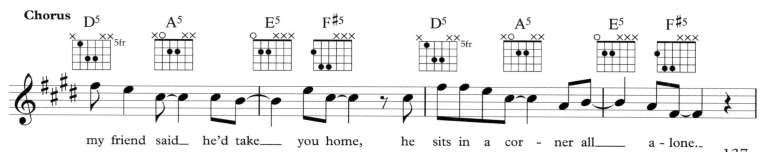

my friend said_ he'd take____ you home, he sits in a cor - ner all____ a - lone._

137

He lives un - der a wa - ter - fall,___ no - bo - dy can see him, no-

- bo - dy can ev - er hear him call, no - bo - dy can ev - er hear him

Guitar Solo

call.

Ah,_____ ah._____ 2. You need to

Coda

call, No - bo - dy can ev - er hear him

Guitar Solo

Repeat to fade

138   call.

Use Somebody

Words & Music by Caleb Followill, Nathan Followill, Jared Followill & Matthew Followill

Verse 2:
Someone like you and all you know and how you speak,
Countless lovers, undercover of the street.
You know that I could use somebody,
You know that I could use somebody.

Verse 3:
Off in the night while you live it up, I'm off to sleep,
Waging wars to shake the poet and the beat.
I hope it's gonna make you notice,
I hope it's gonna make you notice.

Whiskey In The Jar

Traditional

Arranged by Phil Lynott, Brian Downey & Eric Bell

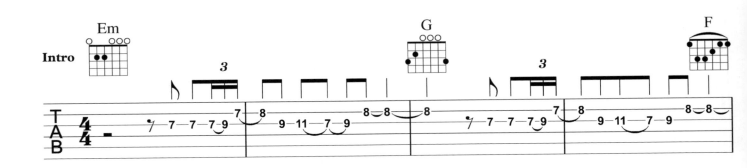

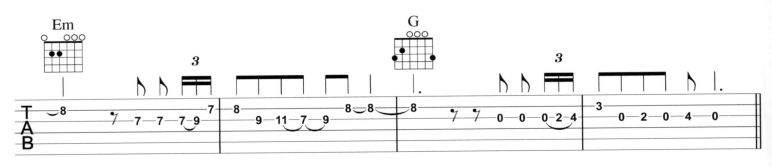

1. As

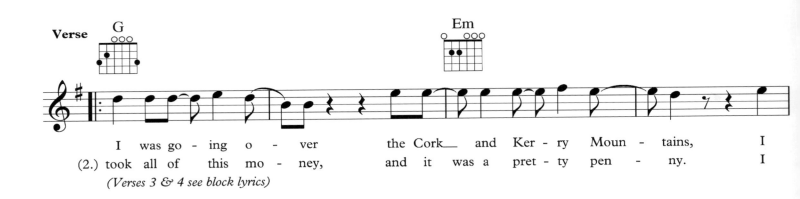

I was go - ing o - ver the Cork__ and Ker - ry Moun - tains, I
(2.) took all of this mo - ney, and it was a pret - ty pen - ny. I

(Verses 3 & 4 see block lyrics)

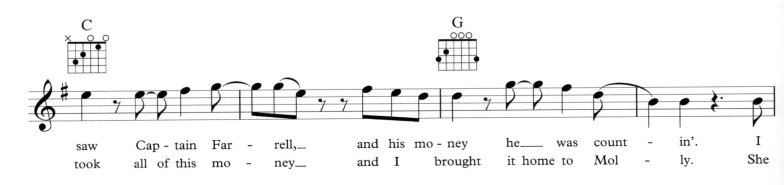

saw Cap - tain Far - rell,__ and his mo - ney he__ was count - in'. I
took all of this mo - ney__ and I brought it home to Mol - ly. She

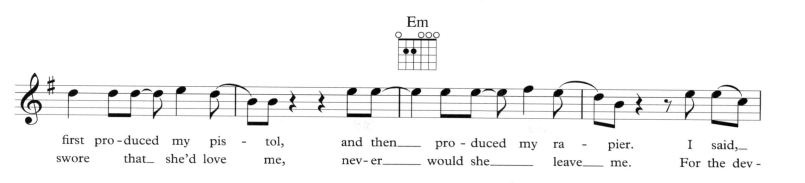

first pro-duced my pis - tol, and then___ pro - duced my ra - pier. I said,___
swore that_ she'd love me,   nev-er___ would she___ leave___ me. For the dev-

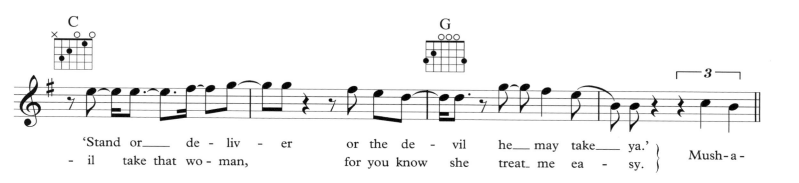

'Stand or___ de - liv - er or the de - vil he__ may take___ ya.' }
- il take that wo - man, for you know she treat_ me ea - sy. } Mush-a-

Chorus

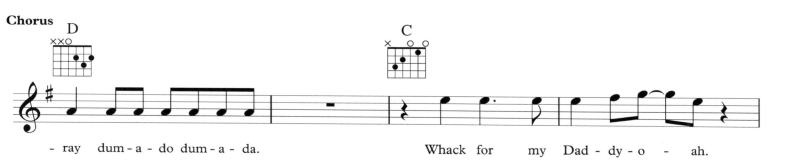

- ray dum - a - do dum - a - da.   Whack for my Dad-dy-o - ah.

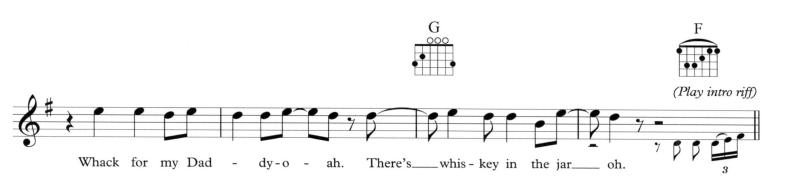

(Play intro riff)

Whack for my Dad - dy-o - ah. There's___whis-key in the jar___ oh.

1-4.

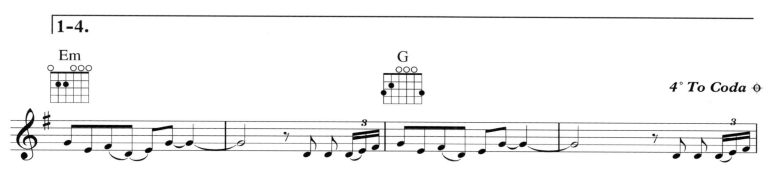

4° To Coda ⊕

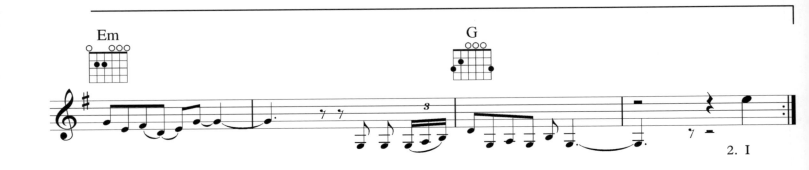

Coda

Repeat sim. to fade

Verse 3
Being drunk and weary
I went to Molly's chamber,
Taking my money with me.
And I never knew the danger,
For 'bout six or maybe seven,
In walked Captain Farrell.
I jumped up, fired off my pistols,
And I shot him with both barrels.

Verse 4
Now, some men like a-fishin',
And some men like a-fowlin',
And some men like to hear
The cannonball a-roarin'.
Me, I like sleepin',
'Specially in my Molly's chamber.
But here I am in prison.
Here I am with a ball and chain, yeah.

Yellow

Words & Music by Guy Berryman, Chris Martin, Jon Buckland & Will Champion

You Really Got Me

Words & Music by Ray Davies

148

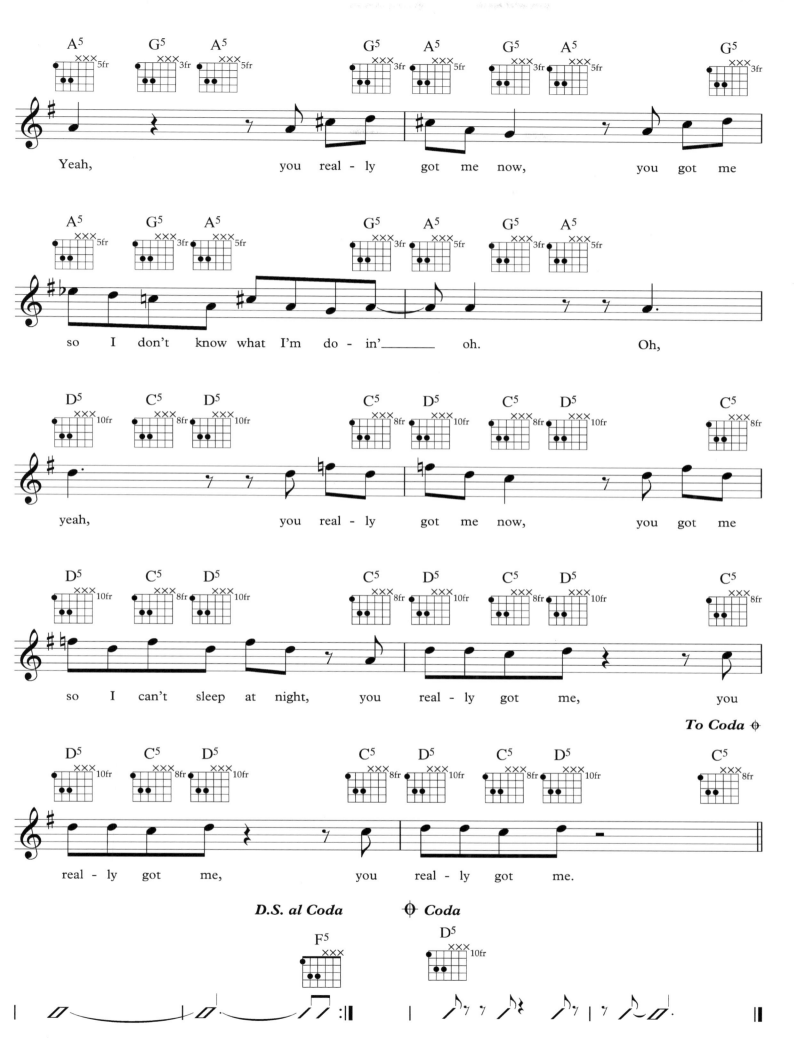

You Shook Me All Night Long

Words & Music by Angus Young, Malcolm Young & Brian Johnson

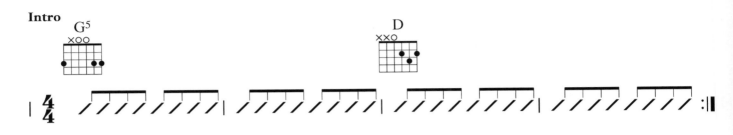

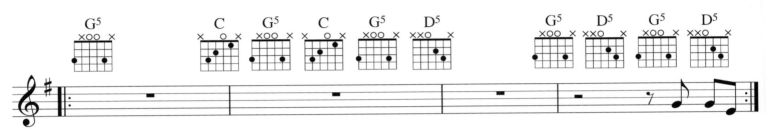

(2° only) 1. She was a

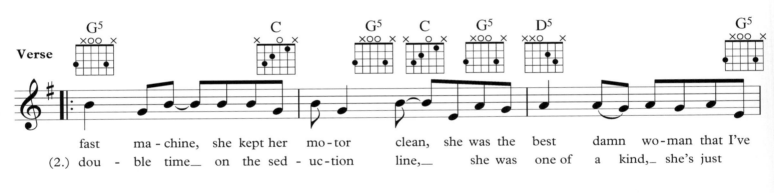

fast ma-chine, she kept her mo-tor clean, she was the best damn wo-man that I've
(2.) dou-ble time__ on the sed-uc-tion line,__ she was one of a kind,__ she's just

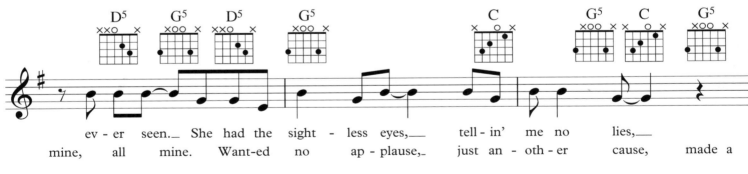

ev-er seen.__ She had the sight-less eyes,__ tell-in' me no lies,__
mine, all mine. Want-ed no ap-plause,__ just an-oth-er cause, made a

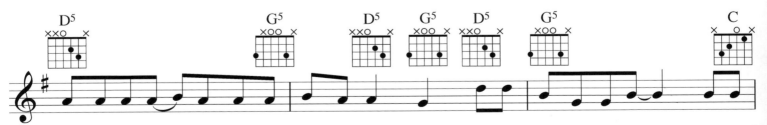

knock-in' me out__ with those Am-er-i-can thighs. Tak-in' more than her share, had me
meal out-ta me and came back for more. Had to cool it down to take an-

fight-in' for air,___ she told me to come_ but I was al-read-y there.__ 'Cause the
- oth-er round,_ now I'm back in the ring__ to take an - oth-er swing._ 'Cause the

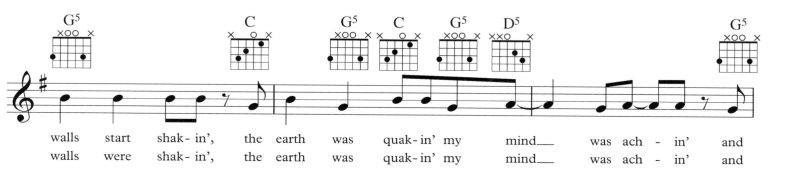

walls start shak-in', the earth was quak-in' my mind__ was ach - in' and
walls were shak-in', the earth was quak-in' my mind__ was ach - in' and

Chorus

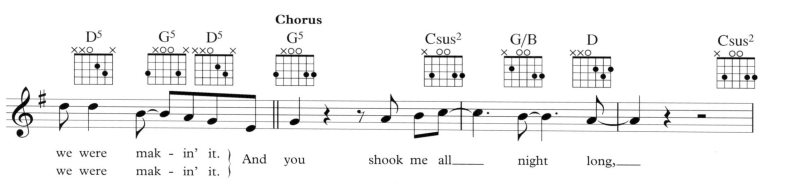

we were mak - in' it. } And you shook me all___ night long,___
we were mak - in' it. }

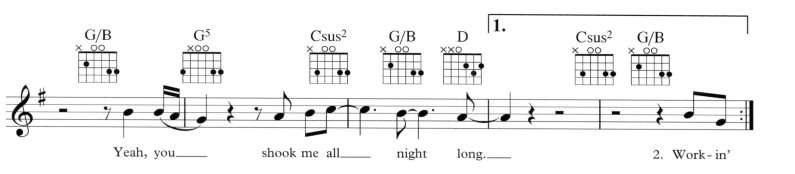

1.

Yeah, you___ shook me all___ night long.___ 2. Work-in'

2.

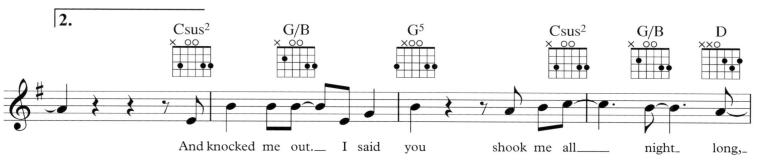

And knocked me out._ I said you shook me all___ night_ long,_

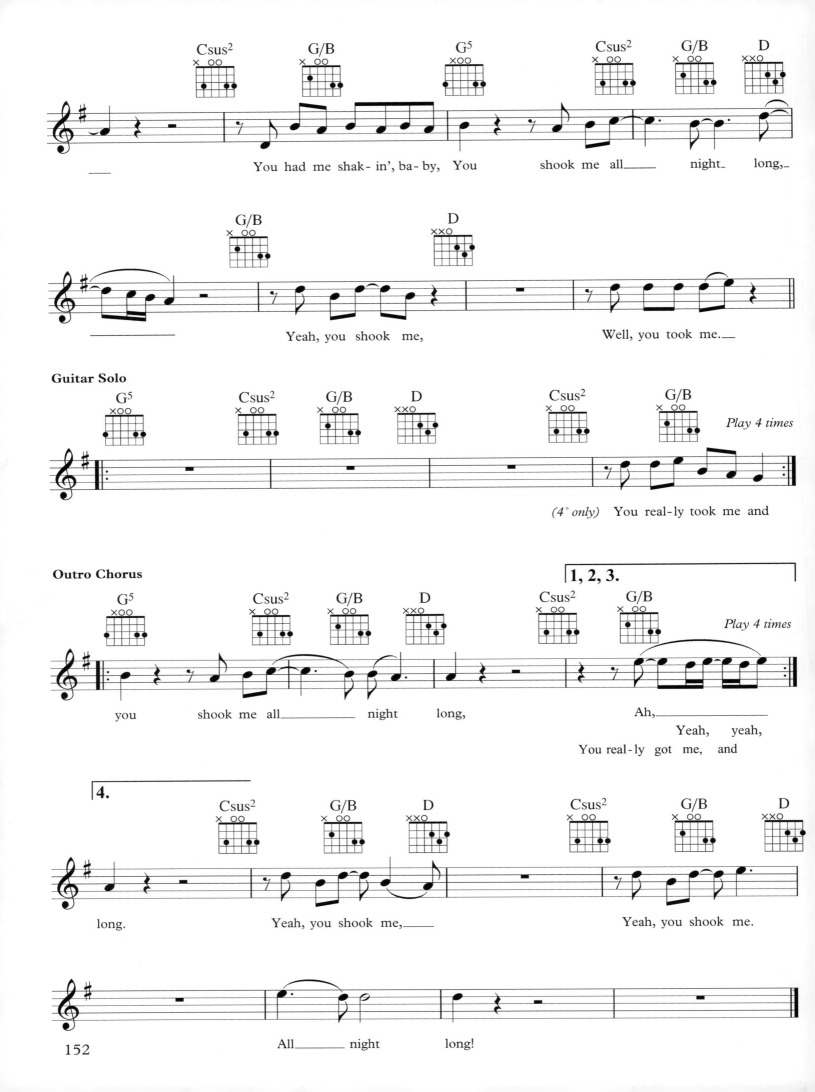

Ziggy Stardust

Words & Music by David Bowie

Intro riff:

Verse

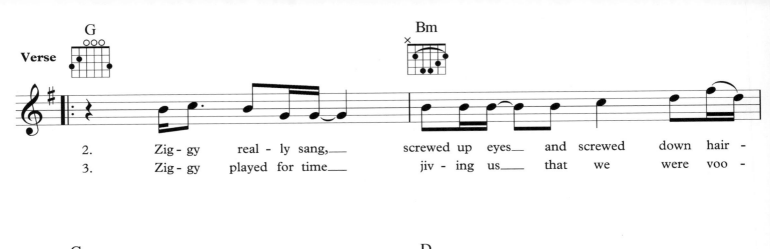

2.   Zig - gy   real - ly sang,___   screwed up eyes__ and screwed   down   hair -
3.   Zig - gy   played for time__   jiv - ing us___ that   we   were   voo -

-do,   like some cat from Ja -   pan.____   He could lick 'em   by smil -
doo,   the__ kids were just   crass.___   He was   the nazz

- ing,   he could leave 'em to hang.__   They came on so load-ed man,   well hung and
with   God giv-en ass.__   He took it all too far__   but boy could he

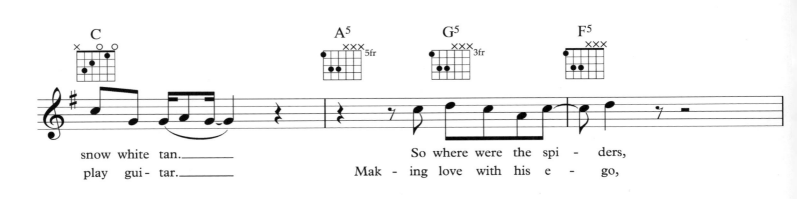

snow white tan._____   So where were the spi -   ders,
play gui - tar._____   Mak - ing love with his e - go,

while the fly tried to break__ our balls?__   With just the beer light to guide__
154   Zig - gy sucked up in - to_____ his mind..   (Ah!)   Like a   lep-er Mes-si -

Zombie

Words & Music by Dolores O'Riordan

Strumming style:

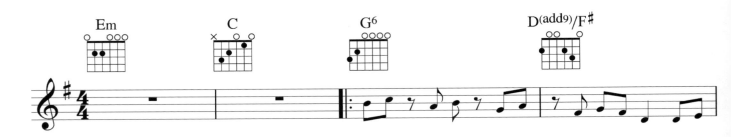

Verse

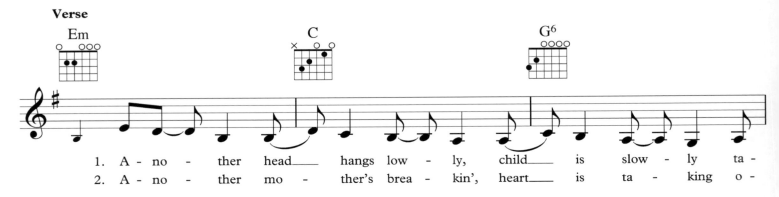

1. A - no - ther head___ hangs low - ly, child___ is slow - ly ta -
2. A - no - ther mo - ther's brea - kin', heart___ is ta - king o -

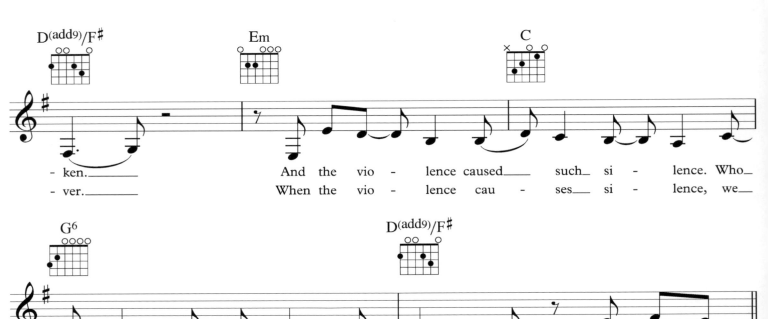

- ken.___ And the vio - lence caused___ such si - lence. Who___
- ver.___ When the vio - lence cau - ses___ si - lence, we___

___ are we___ mis - ta - ken?___ But you see,
___ must be___ mis - ta - ken.___ It's the same

it's not me,   it's not my   fa - mi - ly.
old__ theme   since__ nine - teen- six- teen.   } In your head,__   in your head__ they are fight-

- ing   with their tanks   and their bombs   and their bombs   and their guns.   In your head,__

Chorus

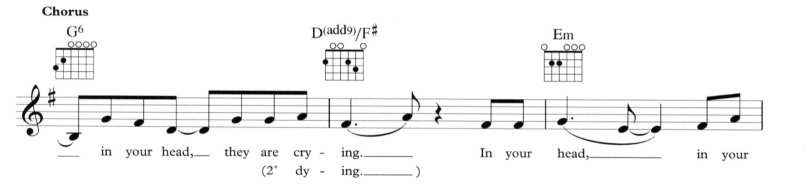

__ in your head,__ they are cry - ing._____   In your head,_____   in your
              (2° dy - ing._____)

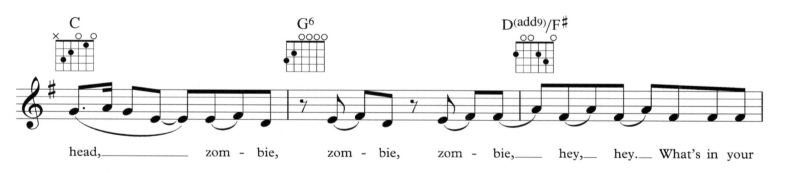

head,_____   zom - bie,   zom - bie,   zom - bie,__ hey,__ hey.__ What's in your

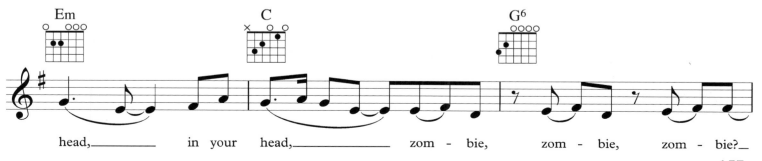

head,_____   in your head,_____   zom - bie,   zom - bie,   zom - bie?__

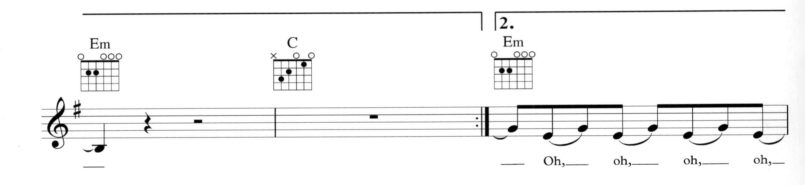

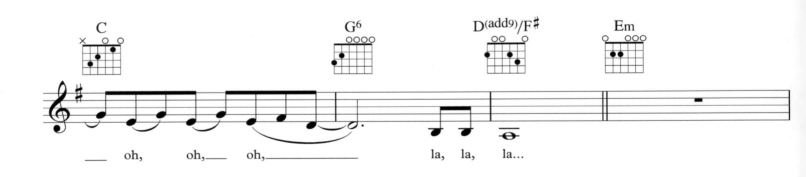

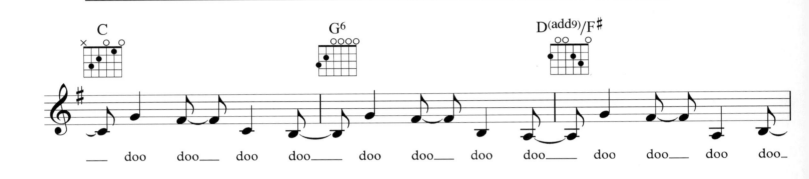

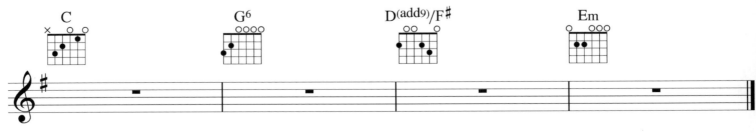

23456789